Archives, Personal Papers, and Manuscripts

A Cataloging Manual

for

Archival Repositories,

Historical Societies, and

Manuscript Libraries

2nd edition

Compiled by

Steven L. Hensen
Manuscript Department
Duke University Library

Society of American Archivists
Chicago

1989

Credits:

This publication was made possible in part by a grant from the Division of Research Programs of the National Endowment for the Humanities, an independent federal agency.

Much of the material found in chapters 2-6 has been reprinted with permission of the American Library Association, excerpts taken from *Anglo-American Cataloguing Rules*, 2nd ed., 1988 revision; copyright 1988, American Library Association.

Library of Congress Catalog Card No. 89-063416
ISBN 0-931828-73-2

CONTENTS

PART I

Description

PART II

Headings and Uniform Titles

Appendices

Preface to the Second Edition

The underlying assumption upon which the first edition of this cataloging manual was based was that the system of library-based cataloging techniques embodied in the second edition of the *Anglo-American Cataloguing Rules* (AACR 2) could be adapted to serve the needs of archival description. This premise, which was viewed with suspicion by many in the archival community, required both that archival description and library cataloging be acknowledged as fundamentally similar and that their differences be recognized and accommodated. It was necessary to demonstrate that these rules were sufficiently sensitive to basic archival principles, and at the same time to establish that the essence of AACR 2 could be preserved within a fundamentally archival framework.

The wide success and acceptance of the first edition has proved the essential validity of that assumption. It is now generally understood by manuscript curators, archivists, and librarians that, while chapter 4 of AACR 2 may still be used for a more bibliographically oriented style of manuscript cataloging, the approaches recommended in *Archives, Personal Papers, and Manuscripts*[1] (or "APPM" as it is now known) are more useful for most modern manuscript and archival description. Furthermore, they have come to be regarded as the standard for most archival bibliographic description. The Library of Congress, the Research Libraries Group, and OCLC all consider machine-readable catalog records prepared according to these rules to be fully compatible with AACR 2.

One of the principal hopes behind the development of the first edition of these rules was that they would encourage archival and manuscript cataloging within what was then termed the "burgeoning national systems for automated bibliographic description."[2] With more than 200,000 records for archival and manuscript material currently in the bibliographic utilities, that hope has been more than realized.

While it is generally acknowledged that the successful integration of these records would not have been possible without the descriptive cataloging framework provided by APPM, this same experience has also revealed certain problem areas.

Although the appearance of the USMARC Archival and Manuscripts Control format (AMC) and APPM in the same year now seems fortuitous, it was actually more coincidental. While the close relationship between descriptive standards and the use of the format is now better understood, at that time there was no conscious attempt to reconcile or coordinate the work of one project with the other. It is not surprising that certain incongruities arose between the rules and the format.

One of the purposes of this edition, then, is to attempt to resolve these problems. Four different approaches have been used:

First, the names and definitions of the descriptive elements have been altered where necessary to conform more closely to the corresponding field in the USMARC format.

Second, equivalent descriptive elements were added for those USMARC fields that were not previously represented and that were considered important for cataloging purposes. This was done to provide guidance in formulating content of fields where none

---

1. *Archives, Personal Papers and Manuscripts: A Cataloging Manual for Archival Repositories, Historical Societies, and Manuscript Libraries* (Washington, D.C.: Library of Congress, 1983).

2. APPM (1983), p. 1.

was previously offered. Not all of the available USMARC fields have been included, particularly where the use of the element was considered to be too infrequent or oriented to local purposes.

Third, areas of identified ambiguity or confusion have been addressed with the intent either to make the guidelines more straightforward or to offer a clearer explanation of application problems.

Fourth, the entire question of the relationship of the USMARC format to various elements of description and headings has been addressed directly, by providing USMARC-oriented explications of certain rules. Where illustrative examples have been given in the rules themselves, coded versions of those examples have been included in Appendix II under the same rule numbers.

In addition, all pertinent rule interpretations issued by the Library of Congress subsequent to the publication of the first edition of this manual have been incorporated where possible. Such interpretations have the force of rules for most U.S. libraries and archives.[3]

Another area of substantial revision is the attempt to broaden the application of archival cataloging. Where the first edition of these rules was limited principally to archival description of textual materials (and microform reproductions of those materials), experience has shown that in actual practice archival description must accommodate many different media. While it is true that the bulk of the holdings of most archives and manuscript repositories may be textual or paper materials (i.e., "language" materials in the terminology of the USMARC format), it is also true that nontextual materials, such as photographs and other graphic materials, motion pictures and videorecordings, sound recordings, and computer files, are found increasingly among archival records and "manuscript" collections. These nontextual materials may form part of a predominantly textual collection or series, or may constitute archival groups of their own.

This edition takes a more global view of archival cataloging and attempts to give many of the rules in chapter 1 a less specifically textual context.

Finally, in the process that is currently underway to integrate the various USMARC formats, making all fields theoretically available for cataloging all types of material, there are obvious implications for descriptive conventions. Manuals like this one must be even more explicit about the limits or parameters of effective cataloging practice and must establish normative standards to guide catalogers.

ADDITION OF PART II, GUIDELINES FOR CHOOSING AND FORMULATING HEADINGS

Concomitant with the general acceptance and adoption of the USMARC AMC format, archivists have found themselves increasingly obliged to accommodate themselves to other library-based bibliographic standards, especially those for choosing, forming, and using bibliographic headings. When AACR 2 was first published, many archivists and manuscript curators found its approach to forming name headings, which was oriented toward author and title page, difficult to understand, if not somewhat antithetical to archival principles. In addition, the lack of any specific guidelines for choosing headings for manuscripts in chapter 21 and the lack of any manuscript-

---

3. Interpretations, expansions, and cancellations of the rules in AACR 2 are published by the Library of Congress in its *Cataloging Service Bulletin* (quarterly) and in *Library of Congress Rule Interpretations*, 2nd ed., 1989 (cumulative edition with quarterly updates).

oriented rules or examples in chapters 22-25 made this a difficult area to address in APPM. In fact, the advice ultimately offered in the first edition was simply to follow AACR 2 as closely as possible and hope for the best. That advice is no longer adequate. Consequently, the other major difference in this edition is the addition in Part II of guidelines for choosing and formulating headings.

The actual experience of archivists over the last four years in using the cataloging rules and in using AACR 2 has proved that some of the anticipated problems were not as great as had been feared. Most of the 200,000 AMC records mentioned above have generally followed and used AACR 2 with a high degree of success. The advantages of integrating bibliographic records for archival materials with those for other library materials have provided a more compelling incentive for cooperation.

The approach followed in this manual in providing guidelines for forming headings has been, first, to select from AACR 2 only those rules considered likely to be encountered most often by archivists and manuscript catalogers in the United States. Because it was often difficult to extract individual rules without their context, the selections are generous. While most common problems are covered, archivists who must deal with the complexities of Thai names, for example, must still consult AACR 2 rule 22.28. As with Part I, Library of Congress rule interpretations have been incorporated where necessary to insure that the guidelines are absolutely consistent with current practice.

Second, where an archival context for a rule is considered necessary, a specific archival orientation, commentary, or interpretation has been provided. These commentaries will be found bracketed ([ ]) and in **bold face** following the rule.

Third, examples from actual archival situations or from existing archival records have been provided to illustrate the usage of a particular rule.

If there are questions regarding any rules given in this section of this manual, catalogers should always consult AACR 2.[4] For further information on the background of the approaches followed here, consult the introduction to Part II.

ORGANIZATION OF THE MANUAL

The design and layout of the second edition of this manual differs somewhat from the first edition. To accommodate the substantial addition of rules governing choice and form of headings to the existing rules on description in a logical and comprehensible form, a new system of chapter and rule numbers has been adopted. Since the first edition was basically a reworking and expansion of chapter 4 of AACR 2, the original rule numbering system was largely preserved. With this edition incorporating additional material selected from chapters 21-25, it was felt that chapters numbered 4, 21, 22, 23, 24, and 25 would be confusing, particularly since this numbering would have occasional gaps.

Thus, this edition is divided--as is AACR 2--into two major parts. Part I relates to description. The single chapter therein, numbered 1, contains rules for the description of archival and manuscript materials and corresponds to chapters 1 and 4 of AACR 2 as well as the greater part of the first edition of APPM. Part II relates to choice and form of headings and uniform titles. It contains chapters with rules covering choice of access points (chapter 2), forming personal name headings (chapter 3), forming geographic name headings (chapter 4), forming corporate name headings (chapter 5), and forming uniform title headings (chapter 6).

---

4. References to AACR 2 here and elsewhere in this manual refer to the 1988 revision: *Anglo-American Cataloguing Rules*, 2nd edition, 1988 revision (Chicago: American Library Association, 1988).

Because the rules in chapters 3-6 consist chiefly of verbatim selections from the equivalent chapters (22-25) and subsequent rule interpretations in AACR 2, specific rule number citations to AACR 2 have been provided in square brackets following each rule. This has been done so that the inevitable questions catalogers will have can be resolved quickly and authoritatively by referring directly to the equivalent AACR 2 rule or interpretation. The presence of a rule interpretation is indicated either by the designation *[RI]* following the paragraph(s) where it appears, or by the heading *Interpretation* (used for longer sections).

It must again be stressed that the rules in these chapters are not exhaustive. They are only *selections* designed to assist archivists and manuscript catalogers in forming headings for the bibliographic descriptions they create. All questions, problems, and special cases regarding headings *must* be resolved using the appropriate chapter in AACR 2.

CHANGES FROM THE FIRST EDITION

In the title area more latitude is now permitted in adding the name element to supplied titles (see 1.1B3).

In the date area specific provisions for adding "bulk dates" are now given (see 1.1B5), and the placement of certain date information has been clarified.

An edition area has been added for individual manuscripts. This was done because of changes approved for chapter 4 of AACR 2.

In the physical description area (see 1.5) there are some new recommendations for recording extent of microforms.

In the note area (see 1.7) there is now more congruity between the various notes and the equivalent USMARC fields. In addition, there is no longer any stated or preferred order of notes. Repositories may record notes in any useful order, although most archivists agree that the scope and content note belongs near the head of the record.

FORM OF HEADINGS USED IN BIBLIOGRAPHIC RECORDS

While the theory and application of subject cataloging to archival description is beyond the scope of this manual, it nevertheless must be pointed out that the form of personal, corporate, and geographic names and uniform titles used as subject headings is governed by the same rules that govern their formation as other headings in a bibliographic record. In other words, the form of a person's name as established under AACR 2 for a main entry is the same form that must be used as an added or subject entry. For guidance in the assignment and structure of topical and other subject headings to manuscript and archival cataloging, see the *Library of Congress Subject Headings*, and the *Library of Congress Subject Cataloging Manual: Subject Headings*.

Acknowledgments

As with the first edition of this work, there have been many significant contributions beyond those of the compiler. Lisa Weber, who was then Automation Program Officer with the Society of American Archivists, originally convinced me that this revision of *Archives, Personal Papers, and Manuscripts* (APPM) was needed. She incorporated funding for it in a proposal to the National Endowment for the Humanities to support the second phase of the SAA's Automation Program. To a large extent, this revision is a direct reflection of the extraordinary vision and energy that Lisa has given to the archival profession over the last few years. When Lisa departed to the National Historical Publications and Records Commission after the beginning of this project, her duties were assumed by Marion Matters. Marion's own enthusiasm and her remarkable feel for editorial details were exactly what was needed to prod this project into completion.

Special thanks must also be given to the Duke University Library (in particular to Robert Byrd, Curator of Manuscripts, and Jerry Campbell, University Librarian) for giving me both the time and the professionally nurturing atmosphere in which to do much of this work. Additional thanks must be given to the Research Libraries Group, which recognized my commitment to finish this project while employed as a consultant and program officer.

The success of the first edition of this manual was due in large measure to the considerable force of the imprimatur of the Library of Congress, in which it was produced and through which it was issued. Without the continued cooperation of the library, this second edition of APPM never would have been started and never would have reached a satisfactory conclusion. Thanks must go to Henriette Avram and Lucia Rather for agreeing to library participation and especially to the LC editorial committee, consisting of Ben Tucker, Harriet Ostroff, Jeffrey Heynen, and Emily Zehmer, for their many important suggestions and insights.

While it has been impossible to respond directly to all those who commented in such useful detail on the first draft of these rules, special thanks should go to Edward Swanson, Jackie Dooley, and Kathleen Roe for providing such extensive and useful comments. The others will see many of their own suggestions reflected in this final version.

Finally, the vital assistance and support of the National Endowment for the Humanities and the Society of American Archivists in underwriting this project must be acknowledged. Also of critical importance has been the encouragement of the American Library Association by permitting extensive direct quotation from the 2nd edition (1988 revision) of the *Anglo-American Cataloguing Rules*.

Steve Hensen
Mountain View, California
July 1989

PART I

DESCRIPTION

Introduction

SCOPE OF THE RULES

0.1. These rules are intended for use in the construction of catalogs by archival repositories, or by libraries or other institutions that wish to provide archivally oriented cataloging for materials that may be among their holdings.[1]

0.2. Research use of archival materials, one of the primary reasons for their preservation, depends upon access to information about them. These rules have been written to permit the integration of information about archival materials with information about other research resources in bibliographic systems. The rules therefore provide guidance for archival cataloging within the general structure and approach of *Anglo-American Cataloguing Rules*, 2nd ed. (AACR 2). This manual is intended to replace chapter 4 of AACR 2 for repositories that wish to emphasize aspects of archival control over bibliographic control in their cataloging (see 0.8 below).

0.3. These rules cover description of the provenance, scope, content, and form of archival material, regardless of physical medium. Terms such as *archival material*, *collection*, and *archival series* are used throughout to refer to either textual or nontextual material. However, for item level description, the rules are textually oriented. This manual may be used for item description of nontextual material, but such material may be better accommodated using other manuals (see 1.0A).

0.4. These rules cover the choice of access points and the forms of headings for names of persons, names of corporate bodies, geographic names, and uniform titles used as access points.

0.5. These rules do not cover either the choice or form of other types of access points (e.g., topical subject, form or genre, function).

0.6. These rules generally do not cover the description of archival management actions (e.g., appraisal, processing, preservation, reference), although the results of those actions may be reflected in the bibliographic descriptions created according to the rules. Information about management actions, although an important aspect of archival control, is presumed to be subject to the requirements of individual repositories.[2]

ARCHIVAL CATALOGS AND OTHER FINDING AIDS

0.7. An archival catalog may be only one part of a more complex institutional descriptive system, which may include several other types of *finding aids* (e.g., registers, inventories,

---

1. The term *repository* will be used throughout to mean any institution holding archival material.

2. Continuing experiments in sharing appraisal data may in the future provide both the rationale and agreement on common practice required for standardization of description in this area.

calendars, indexes, and shelf and container lists).[3] In such a system, a catalog record created according to these rules is usually a summary or abstract of information contained in other finding aids, which in turn contain summaries, abstracts, or lists based on information found in the archival materials themselves. There is no requirement, however, that an archival catalog record be an abstract of a more substantial finding aid. The finding aid and the catalog record may be equivalent when the nature of the materials and repository policy dictate a summary approach to description of individual collections or entire holdings.

ARCHIVAL DESCRIPTION

0.8. Archival description or cataloging, as prescribed in this manual, is based on certain assumptions about the nature of archival materials and the way archivists manage them.

1) Their significance is heavily dependent on the context of their creation, i.e., their *provenance*.
2) They most often exist in groups or collectivities and are managed at the collective level.
3) They are often unique, generally "unpublished," usually generated as documentary byproducts of certain kinds of human activity.

With these assumptions as background, a cataloger would use this manual to create a record that exemplifies *archival control*, rather than *bibliographic control*, over the materials described. The process of archival cataloging consists predominantly of *interpreting*, *extrapolating*, or *extracting* information from the material and its context.[4]

0.9. *Provenance*. Archival materials are created as the natural byproduct, or record, of the activities or functions of persons or corporate bodies. Such materials are often said to be generated organically. The arrangement and description of these materials according to their original function or purpose (often known as *respect du fonds*) is a fundamental principle of modern archival science. Respect for the original provenance of archival materials guarantees their essential integrity and historical accuracy and also preserves the evidential value inherent in the original grouping and ordering of materials. In some cases, however, archivists also deal with artificial gatherings or collections that have been assembled by others without regard for the provenance or origin of individual pieces. The intent of the collector, often reflected in a focus or theme, may provide contextual meaning for the pieces.

> *Effect on cataloging rules*: Guidelines for choice of entry reflect the relationship between archival provenance and responsibility; thus rules for entry under corporate name, especially, are different from those in AACR 2. The rules also provide for the following important notes: biographical or historical sketches con-

---

3. Although this manual does not directly address questions relating to the standard practices of arrangement and description which produce these finding aids, a clear understanding of the proper context and relationship of cataloging to these practices is fundamental and inherent in all the rules that follow. For more information regarding these practices, see Frederic Miller, *Arranging and Describing Archives* (working title) to be published by the Society of American Archivists in 1990.

4. By contrast, a bibliographic approach is characterized by item oriented cataloging to provide a description, usually of a published item, as a physical entity. The cataloging process consists predominantly of *transcribing* information that appears on or with the item.

cerning the creator (personal or corporate) of the materials; substantial scope and content analysis; organization and arrangement; and custodial history and source(s) of acquisition.

0.10. *Collective description.* This manual approaches the problems of archival cataloging principally at the collection level for two reasons:

1) Collection level description supports the principles of archival unity.
   These principles assume that in most organically generated collections the significance of the individual component (subseries, file, document, etc.) lies primarily in its relation to the collective whole. The significance of the whole derives from interrelationships among its components. Emphasis on individual components at the expense of the whole collection may tend to obscure the intrinsic importance of the whole.

2) Collection level description is practical.
   With modern archival collections consisting of tens and hundreds of thousands of items, an item level approach would impose overwhelming cataloging burdens. Most archivists believe that comprehensive summary control of their holdings at the collection level is preferable to detailed control of only a part.

Effect on cataloging rules: Rules reflect the fact that the cataloger almost always must supply a title for a collection, and that a collection's inclusive dates are considered an integral part of its title. Supplied titles are *not* enclosed in square brackets. Rules for physical description allow expression of the amount of *space* (linear or cubic feet) or number of *containers* occupied by a collection, as well as expression of the number of physical pieces in a collection.

0.11. *"Unpublished" material.* Whether an unselfconscious byproduct of human activity or a "work" of conscious accumulation or documentation, an archival collection generally lacks the formally presented identifying data that characterize most published items, such as author and title statements, imprints, production and distribution information, collation, etc. Personal or corporate responsibility for the creation of archival materials (another way of saying provenance) is generally inferred from, rather than explicitly stated in the materials. Titles are supplied rather than transcribed by the cataloger. If there is a practical equivalent to the bibliographic title page, it is the archival finding aid (of the inventory or register type), which is based on analysis of the collection itself, on accession records, and on reference sources.

Effect on cataloging rules. The concepts of "chief source of information" and "prescribed source of information" that guide bibliographic cataloging must be applied to different sources in archival cataloging. Rules concerning date, edition, and title reflect the fact that this information is not normally available for literal transcription.

LEVELS OF DESCRIPTION

0.12. There may be several appropriate levels of description for any given body of archival material. These levels normally correspond to natural divisions based on provenance or physical form. The principle corresponds with the bibliographic concept of *analysis*, "the process of preparing a bibliographic record that describes a part or parts of an item for which a comprehensive entry has been made."[5] Description of an archival subunit is done within the context of a hierarchically superior unit--*for which a comprehensive entry has been made*--so that a folder level record will refer to and clearly be subordinate to the record for the subseries of which it is a part, the subseries record to the series record, and so on.[6] What is important is that, for any particular body of archival material, there should be a record at the most comprehensive level if there are to be additional records at any subordinate level.

0.13. These rules may be used for description at any level where the objective is to provide access through separate catalog records. The intent is to give archival catalog records a consistent format at every level, from the most comprehensive to the smallest component. The *choice* of level(s) appropriate to individual collections or entire repository holdings must be made by each repository based on its own internal needs.

---

5. AACR 2 rule 13.1A.

6. The number of levels in such a hierarchy is *not* prescribed. Archivists following the National Archives model may refer to a five-level hierarchy (from most comprehensive to least): record group, subgroup, series, subseries, file unit (e.g., folder). Others may use a different sequence of terms for a similar hierarchy (from most comprehensive to least): collection, series, subseries, file unit (e.g., folder), document or item.

CHAPTER 1

DESCRIPTION OF ARCHIVAL MATERIAL

Contents

---

* Not defined for archival usage.

1.0. GENERAL RULES

1.0A. Scope. The rules in this chapter cover the description of archival materials (as defined in the introduction), regardless of physical form or medium. Such materials may consist of collections, single manuscripts, or archival record groups and record series as defined below.[1]

> **Manuscript/Document**. Any text in handwriting or typescript (including printed forms completed by hand or typewriter) which may or may not be part of a collection of such texts. Examples of manuscripts and documents are letters, diaries, ledgers, minutes, speeches, marked or corrected galley or page proofs, manuscript books, and legal papers. For the purpose of this manual, these materials may exist in original handwritten or typescript form, letter-press or carbon copies, or photographic or mechanical reproduction, including photostat, microform, or facsimile.

> **Series**. File units or documents arranged in accordance with a filing system or maintained as a unit because they relate to a particular subject or function, result from the same activity, have a particular form, or because of some other relationship arising out of their creation, receipt, or use. Also known as *record series*. In archival practice, the series is the usual unit of cataloging or description.

---

1. For additional definitions of archives and manuscripts terminology, see "A Basic Glossary for Archivists, Manuscript Curators, and Records Managers," by Frank B. Evans and others, *American Archivist* 37 (July 1974): 415-431. In 1990 the Society of American Archivists plans to publish a new glossary, *The Vocabulary of Archives and Manuscripts* (working title), compiled by Lewis and Lynn Bellardo.

Collection. A body of archival material formed by or around a person, family group, corporate body, or subject either from a common source as a natural product of activity or function, or gathered purposefully and artificially without regard to original provenance. In addition to the types of manuscript material listed above, a collection may also contain correspondence, memoranda, photographs, maps, drawings, near-print materials, pamphlets, periodical tear-sheets, broadsides, newspaper clippings, motion picture films, computer files, etc.

Record group. A body of organizationally related archives or records established on the basis of provenance with particular regard for the administrative history, the complexity, and the volume of the records and archives of the institution or organization involved.

Archives. The preserved documentary records of any corporate body, governmental agency or office, or organization or group that are the direct result of administrative or organizational activity of the originating body and that are maintained according to their original provenance.

Alternatively, manuscript cartographic items, manuscript music, certain pre-1600 manuscripts, codices, and nontextual archival materials such as graphics (including photographs), computer files, and motion pictures and videorecordings may be cataloged according to other rules.[2] This is true whether or not such materials are part of a larger group of archival materials. In some cases a cataloger may consult other rules manuals for guidance in providing medium-specific detail (particularly in the physical description and note areas) while the description as a whole follows *this* manual. In other cases, a cataloger may choose to follow other rules for the entire description. Decisions about when to use other rules may be made by the cataloger (or by a repository as a whole) based on the characteristics of a particular body of material, the characteristics of certain types of materials, or the requirements of an individual catalog.

1.0B. SOURCES OF INFORMATION

1.0B1. Chief source of information

The chief source of information for archival materials is the finding aid prepared for those materials. In the absence of this source, treat provenance and accession records, then the materials themselves, supplemented by appropriate reference sources, as the chief source of information. For a single item, treat the item itself as the chief source of information. Within a single item, prefer information found on the title page, caption, heading, and colophon (if any). Otherwise, use the text itself, along with its form and

---

2. For book-like manuscripts (e.g., literary manuscripts and codices) and other manuscript material for which a more bibliographically oriented description may be desirable, see chapter 4 of AACR 2 and *Bibliographic Description of Rare Books* (Washington, D.C.: Library of Congress, 1981); for photographs and other graphic material, see chapter 8 of AACR 2 and Elisabeth Betz, *Graphic Materials: Rules for Describing Original Items and Historical Collections* (Washington, D.C.: Library of Congress, 1982); for motion pictures and videorecordings, see chapter 7 of AACR 2 and Wendy White-Hensen, *Archival Moving Image Materials: A Cataloging Manual* (Washington, D.C. [1984]); for maps and cartographic material, see chapter 3 of AACR 2 and *Cartographic Materials: A Manual of Interpretation for AACR 2* (Chicago: American Library Association, 1982); for machine-readable and computer files, see chapter 9 of AACR 2, Sue A. Dodd, *Cataloging Machine-Readable Data Files* (Chicago: American Library Association, 1982), and Sue A. Dodd and Ann M. Sandberg-Fox, *Cataloging Microcomputer Files: A Manual of Interpretation for AACR 2* (Chicago: American Library Association, 1985).

content. If the necessary information is not available from any of these sources, take it from the following sources (in this order of preference):

a) other published or unpublished descriptions of the collection/item
b) reference sources
c) another manuscript copy of the collection/item
d) a published edition of the collection/item
e) other sources

1.0B2. Prescribed sources of information
The prescribed source(s) of information for each area of description of archival and manuscript material is set out below.

AREA	*PRESCRIBED SOURCES OF INFORMATION*
Title and statement of responsibility	Chief source of information
Date	Chief source of information
Edition	Chief source of information and manuscript or published copies
Physical description	Any source
Notes	Any source

1.0C. Punctuation. Each area or each occurrence of an area will normally begin a new paragraph. Otherwise, precede each area, other than the first area, or each occurrence of a note, area, etc., by a period, space, dash, space (. --).[3] For the prescribed punctuation of elements within each area, see the following rules.

Precede each mark of prescribed punctuation by a space and follow it by a space, except for the comma, period, hyphen, and opening and closing parentheses and square brackets. The comma, period, hyphen, and closing parenthesis and square bracket are not preceded by a space; the hyphen and the opening parenthesis and square bracket are not followed by a space.

Exception. Do not precede colons used following introductory wording with a space; similarly, do not precede semicolons used as subelement punctuation with a space.

Indicate an interpolation or extrapolation (i.e., data taken from outside the prescribed source(s) of information) by enclosing it in square brackets ([]). Indicate a conjectural interpolation by adding a question mark within the square brackets. Indicate the omission of part of an element by the mark of omission (...). Precede and follow the mark of omission by a space. Omit any area or element that does not apply in describing an individual item or collection; also omit its prescribed preceding or enclosing punctuation. Do not indicate the omission of an area or element by the mark of omission.

[1897 Jan. 21]

---

3. This punctuation follows general ISBD (International Standard Bibliographic Description) principles. Although there is currently no specific ISBD for archival material, and this punctuation is not customarily followed by archival catalogers, it may be used as a space saving device and to ease integration of archival records with records for printed materials.

[1921?] Mar. 3

Journaal of dag register van den beginne ... , 1780-1784

When adjacent elements within one area are to be enclosed in square brackets, enclose them in one set of square brackets. See also 1.0F.

[1.0C1]

[1835 Nov. 1, Sumter District, S.C.]

1.0D. Levels of detail in the description. The elements of description provided in the rules in this entire chapter constitute a maximum set of information. This particular rule sets out two recommended levels of description and the elements necessary to each level. Archival repositories may choose only the first level, or the first and second, based on the purpose of the catalog or catalogs for which the entry is constructed. Include this minimum set of elements for all items cataloged at the chosen level when the elements are applicable to the unit being described and when, in the case of *optional additions*, the repository has chosen to include an optional element. Consult individual rules in this chapter for the content of the elements to be included.

1.0D1. First level of detail. This level should include as a minimum: a title statement, with date or inclusive dates; and a statement of quantity or extent. See 1.1B, 1.5, and chapter 2.

> **[In archival cataloging this would apply primarily to very brief records (e.g., accession-level descriptions). Since few bodies of archival material have a "formal" title and statement of responsibility (i.e., one that can be transcribed from the material), a cataloger must supply a title statement (incorporating the form of material) and a statement of extent. The cataloger usually also supplies a main entry (provenance heading). In most USMARC cataloging the only fields that are absolutely required are the title (field 245) and quantity (field 300).]**

1.0D2. Second level of detail. For this level, include all the elements set out in the following rules that are applicable to the material being cataloged.

> **[Most archival cataloging will be done at this second level of detail.]**

1.0E. Language and script of the description. In the title and statement of responsibility area, give information transcribed from the material itself in the language and script (wherever practical) in which it appears there. In all areas prefer the language of the finding aid where the materials it describes are in a different language.

Replace symbols or other matter that cannot be reproduced by the typographical facilities available with a cataloger's description in square brackets.

In general, give interpolations into these areas in the language and script of the other data in the area.

[1.0E]

1.0F. Inaccuracies and extrapolations. In an area where transcription from the item is required, transcribe an inaccuracy or a misspelled word as it appears on the material. Supply a missing letter or letters, number or numbers enclosed in square brackets. Likewise with extrapolations and conjectures, supply the missing information enclosed in square brackets and add the abbreviation *ca.* or a question mark, where appropriate. If a piece of data is being questioned but there is no correction, add a question mark to the data and enclose it in square brackets. See also 1.0C.

[1.0F1]

> [1857 Jan. 3]
> > (*Entire date has been supplied from internal evidence*)
>
> [1864?] Dec. 1
> > (*Probable year has been supplied*)
>
> to Mr. [David?] Smith
> > (*Forename* David *is not given and is supplied*)
>
> Charleston, S.C. [?]
> > (Charleston, S.C. *is given in the source but is questioned by the cataloger on the basis of other evidence*)

If possible, give the correct or properly spelled word directly in the transcription.

> Sop[h]ie's choice
>
> Jam[e]s A. Garfield
> > (*Appears in ms. as* Jams A. Garfield)
>
> Abra[ha]m Linco[l]n
> > (*Appears in ms. as* Abram Lincon)

If this is not possible, insert the correction immediately after the incorrect or mis-spelled word, introduced by *i.e.*

> Pophie's [i.e., Sophie's] choice
>
> ALS, 1829 [i.e., 1830] Jan. 4
> > (*Year was incorrectly given on ms.*)

Exception: If the correct or properly spelled word is perfectly obvious, or if the questionable word is not clearly wrong (as with colloquial usages) add [*sic*] after the transcription.

> Frranklin [sic] D. Roosevelt papers
>
> Sophie's cherce [sic]

1.0G. Accents and other diacritical marks. Add accents and other diacritical marks that are omitted from data found in the source of information in accordance with the usage of the language used in the context.

[1.0G]

1.1. TITLE AND STATEMENT OF RESPONSIBILITY AREA

Contents:

12

1.1E   Other title information
1.1F   Statements of responsibility
1.1G   Items without a collective title

1.1A. Preliminary rule

1.1A1. Punctuation

For instructions on the use of spaces before and after prescribed punctuation, see 1.0C.

Precede each parallel title by an equals sign.

Precede each unit of other title information by a colon.

Precede the first statement of responsibility by a diagonal slash.

Precede each subsequent statement of responsibility by a semicolon.

1.1B. Title proper

1.1B1. Formal title. If a single archival item (such as a manuscript of a speech, article, book, or poem) or an archival collection or record series bears a title as a caption, header, etc., consider this a formal title. Record this formal title exactly as to wording, order, and spelling, but not necessarily as to punctuation or capitalization, and add the date (see 1.1B5). Record formal titles of microforms of manuscript material as above, preferring original titles to titles created in the course of microform publication. In the absence of an original formal title, consider publication title as a formal title.

> Sophie's choice, 1979
>
> Christian ethics and precepts, 1846-1852

1.1B2. Supplied titles. Since most archival material lacks a formal bibliographic title, a title statement must usually be supplied by the cataloger. This statement is established either from a previously prepared descriptive inventory or finding aid (if one exists) or from direct examination of the material. Since these descriptions fall within the definitions under chief and prescribed sources of information (see 1.0B1-1.0B2), do not put titles supplied from these sources in square brackets, except in the case of date(s) actually missing from, or in error on, the material (see 1.1B5).

1.1B3. Name element. *Optionally*, give the name of the person, family, or corporate body predominantly associated with, or responsible for, the collection or item as part of the title statement, unless the name is more appropriately recorded in the statement of responsibility area (see 1.1F). Give the name in direct order natural language. It may be abbreviated if the full name appears elsewhere in the record. If the collection consists of material of two or more persons or families, use all of the names primarily associated with the creation of the collection in the name element. See examples of titles, following rule 1.1B5.

1.1B4. Form of material. Record a term that most specifically characterizes the form of material in the unit being cataloged.

For individual textual items[4] such as literary manuscripts, manuscript volumes (e.g., diaries, journals, orderly books, letter books, account books, ledgers), letters, speeches, sermons, lectures, and legal and financial documents, give the form of material term that is most specific and appropriate for the material cataloged.[5]

> Letter
>
> Diary
>
> Ledger
>
> Lecture

For collections containing a single form of material use an appropriate plural form of material designation.

> Letters
>
> Photographs
>
> Correspondence
>
> Legal documents
>
> Writs of capias ad respondum

For collections consisting of two specific forms of material, each may be given.

> Letter and diploma
>
> Diaries and drawings

For collections, record groups, or series containing multiple forms of material, use the following general terms: *Papers*, for collections of personal papers; *Records*, for the archives of corporate bodies or groups; *Collection* or *Collection of papers*, for any group of materials that was formed artificially around a person, subject, or activity and that otherwise lacks integrity and unity of provenance. When such general titles are used, enumerate specific forms of material in a note if desired (see 1.7B2).

> Records, 1917-1967
>
> Papers, 1888-1920
>
> Collection, 1787-1826

---

4. For cataloging individual nontextual archival items, see the appropriate alternate rules noted above.

5. The following terms and abbreviations may be substituted for *letter, document, manuscript*, etc., as appropriate:
  ALS--autograph letter(s) signed (in the hand of the author)
  LS--letter(s) signed (signature only in the hand of the author)
  TLS--typed letter(s) signed (by the author)
  TL--typed letter(s) (lacking handwritten signature)
  ADS--autograph document(s) signed (by the writer of the text)
  DS--document(s) signed (signature only in the hand of the author)
  holograph(s)--manuscript(s) handwritten by the author
  ms.--any handwritten manuscript
  mss.--plural of ms.; a group of handwritten manuscripts
  typescript(s)--typewritten manuscript(s)
For other authorized abbreviations, see AACR 2, Appendix B.

If appropriate or desirable, add a descriptive modifying term or phrase (e.g., reflecting function, activity, subject area, location, or theme) to the form of material designation (e.g., *Congressional* papers, *Family* papers, *North Carolina* diaries).

> Family papers
>
> Financial aid files
>
> Indenturing committee meeting minutes
>
> Drug investigation correspondence
>
> Medical history files
>
> Autograph collection
>
> Drawings of barns
>
> Videotapes of campaign speeches
>
> Capital equipment inventory computer files

1.1B5. Date. For an archival collection give the inclusive or span dates of the material. For a single item, give the exact date (expressed as year, month, day).[6] Always give the date as the last element in the title.

If the item lacks explicit date information or the information is incomplete and date information must be supplied from internal evidence or from an external source, enclose it in square brackets.[7] If the date information is incomplete and the missing components cannot be supplied, use *no year, no month,* or *no day*, as appropriate. If no date or approximate date can be established (i.e., if even the century is uncertain) use *undated*.

For groups of material subject to continuing additions or accretions, give the inclusive dates as the earliest date of the material followed by a hyphen and *ongoing* in square brackets.

> Special charge vouchers, 1940-[ongoing]

Optionally, add to the inclusive dates of collections or records series, the bulk dates (i.e., the dates for which the materials bulk largest or are most significant), if known. Inclusive dates always take precedence over bulk dates and bulk dates are never entered without inclusive dates. Give the bulk dates in parentheses following the inclusive dates; precede the dates by the word *bulk*.

> Papers, 1703-1908 (bulk 1780-1835)

---

6. For authorized abbreviations of months, see AACR 2, Appendix B.

7. Guidelines for recording probable and uncertain dates:

[1892?]	Probable date
[ca. 1892]	Approximate date
[not before 1875]	Terminal date
[not after 1916 July 16]	Terminal date
[1814 or 1815]	One year or the other
[between 1906 and 1913]	Use only for dates less than 20 years apart
[189-]	Decade certain
[189-?]	Decade uncertain
[18--]	Century certain
[18--?]	Century uncertain

EXAMPLES OF TITLES

Personal papers:

Hamilton, Alexander, 1757-1804. [*Main entry*]
Papers, 1703-1908 (bulk 1780-1835).

Optionally:

Hamilton, Alexander, 1757-1804.
Alexander Hamilton papers, 1703-1908 (bulk 1780-1835).
(*Name element:* Alexander Hamilton)
(*Form of material:* papers)

Flanner, Janet, 1892- [*Main entry*]
Janet Flanner-Solita Solano papers, 1870-1975.

Dumont, Henry, 1878-1949. [*Main entry*]
Henry and Nina Webster Dumont papers, 1905-1936.

Family papers:

Schramm family. [*Main entry*]
Papers, 1932-1971.

Richardson, James Burchell. [*Main entry*]
Family papers, 1803-1910.

Short-Harrison-Symmes family papers, 1760-1878. [*Main entry under title*]

Corporate records:

Bollingen Foundation. [*Main entry*]
Records, 1939-1973.

Optionally:

Bollingen Foundation. [*Main entry*]
Bollingen Foundation records, 1939-1973.
or
Records of the Bollingen Foundation, 1939-1973.

United States. Office of the Comptroller of the Currency. Examining Division. [*Main entry*]
Records, 1863-1935.

Northwestern University (Evanston, Ill). Office of Student Aid. [*Main entry*]
Financial aid files, 1955-1965.

New York (State). Supreme Court of Judicature (Albany). [*Main entry*]
Assignments of error, 1837-1847 (bulk 1837-1839, 1844-1847).

Minnesota. State Board of Corrections and Charities.
  Lantern slides of poorhouses, [190-].

Alabama. Board of Social Work Examiners.
  Expired/inactive license computer files, 1977-[ongoing].

Collections:

Porter, John K. (John Kilham), 1819-1892, *collector*. [*Main entry*]
  Autograph collection, 1600-1882.

Optionally:

Porter, John K. (John Kilham), 1819-1892, *collector*.
  John K. Porter autograph collection, 1600-1882.

Purland, Theodosius, *collector*. [*Main entry*]
  Collection of papers on mesmerism, 1842-1854.

Harkness collection, 1525-1651. [*Main entry under title*]

Shaker collection, 1792-1937. [*Main entry under title*]

Portuguese manuscripts collection, 1345-1918. [*Main entry under title*]

California travel diaries, 1849-1851. [*Main entry under title*]

Single form of material collections:

Correspondence, 1804-1828.

Diaries, [1897?]-1915.

Single manuscripts:

Logbook, 1818-[ca.1823].

Ebenezer Sprout-William Shepard orderly book, 1779-1780.

Diary, 1789 Jan. 1-1791 Mar. 17.

Sutherland, Alan D., 1897- *interviewee*. [*Main entry*]
  Typewritten transcript of oral history interview : Brattleboro, Vt.,
with John Duffy and Martin Kaufman, 1968 June 15.

1.1C. General material designation

1.1C1. Optionally, in a mixed catalog, add, immediately following the title proper, the appropriate general material designation (e.g., *computer file, manuscript, microform, motion picture, picture, sound recording, videorecording*). For the use of other general material designations, see AACR 2 rule 1.1C1. General material designations are always enclosed in square brackets.

1.1D. Parallel titles

1.1D1. For the purposes of this manual, a parallel title shall be defined as a title proper appearing in another language or script on an archival item that has an identifiable title page or its equivalent. Record any parallel titles in the order indicated by their sequence on, or by the layout of, the title page.

[1.1D]

> Twenty love poems and a song of despair = 20 poemas de amor y una canción desesperada, 1976

1.1E. Other title information

1.1E1. Record any title information, other than title proper or parallel titles, appearing on material. This may include subtitles and phrases appearing in conjunction with the title proper or parallel titles indicating the character, contents, etc., of the material or the occasion and/or motive for its production. For single items this may also include place of writing or delivery, addressee, and place to which written. Record other title information following any title proper, parallel title, form title, etc., and before the date(s).

[1.1E]

> Lecture : Royal College of Medicine, London, [18--]
>
> Letter : Dublin, to Henrik Ibsen, Kristiania [Oslo], 1901 Mar. 6
>
> ALS : Worcester Park, Surrey, to George Gissing, Rome, [ca. 1898 Jan. 1]
>
> Holograph petition : to James Monroe, 1813 July 1

When an item or collection has a formal or traditional title, add any form of material information required to make the form and/or nature of the material clear. Punctuate this information as other title information (see also 1.1E). Make this addition after any subtitles or other information.

> Sophie's choice : holograph, 1979
>
> Diamond Lil : playscript, 1928
>
> Christian ethics and precepts : commonplace book, 1846-1852
>
> The need of redirected rural schools : address before the Iowa State Teachers Association, Des Moines : typescript, 1910 Oct. 4

1.1F. Statements of responsibility. Record an explicit statement of responsibility appearing in conjunction with a formal title on the title page of a single manuscript in the form in which it appears there. *Do not* use the statement of responsibility for collections of manuscripts or archival records or for the signers of letters or other documents.

[1.1F]

> The charity ball : a comedy in four acts : typescript, 1889 / by David Belasco and Henry C. DeMille
>
> Divorce : holograph, [187-?] / by Augustin Daly

[Statements of responsibility are used infrequently in archival cataloging, since they seldom exist in collections of material or individual letters or

documents, and, according to AACR 2 rule 1.1F2, must not be constructed nor extracted in the absence of a prominent statement in the item.]

1.1G. Items without a collective title. If two or more manuscripts with formal titles are bound together, form a recognized collection, or are otherwise associated for cataloging purposes and lack a collective formal title, apply the rules for supplying titles to collections as outlined under 1.1B2-1.1B5.

1.2. EDITION AREA

Contents:
1.2A	Preliminary rule
1.2B	Edition statement
1.2C	Statements of responsibility relating to the edition

1.2A. Preliminary rule

1.2A1. Scope. Use this area in item level description to record statements relating to versions of manuscript works existing in two or more versions or states in single or multiple copies. Examples are different manuscript drafts of a work and filmscripts existing in various versions.

[4.2A1]

1.2A2. Punctuation.

For instructions on the use of spaces before or after prescribed punctuation, see 1.0C.
Precede this area by a period, space, dash, space (. --).
Precede the first statement of responsibility following an edition statement by a diagonal slash.
Precede each subsequent statement of responsibility by a semicolon.

[4.2A2]

1.2B. Edition statement

1.2B1. Transcribe a statement relating to a version of a manuscript that is different from other versions, or that is a named revision, as found on the item. Use standard abbreviations (see AACR 2, Appendix B) and numerals in place of words (see AACR 2, Appendix C).

[4.2B1]

Prelim. draft

1st script

2nd draft continuity

Estimating script

1.2B2. In case of doubt as to whether a statement is an edition statement, do not treat it as such.

[4.2B2]

1.2B3. *Optional addition.* If an item lacks an edition statement but is known to contain significant changes from previous versions, supply a suitable brief statement in the language and script of the title proper and enclose it in square brackets.

[4.2B3]

> [2nd draft]
>
> [3. Konzept]
>
> [Continuity]
>
> [Mar. 1970 draft]
>
> [Rev. screenplay]

1.2C. Statements of responsibility relating to the edition

1.2C1. Record a statement of responsibility relating to one or more versions but not to all versions as instructed in 1.1F.

[4.2C1]

> Continuity / written by Waldemar Young
>
> 3rd draft / edited by Paul Watson

1.2C2. In case of doubt about whether a statement of responsibility applies to all versions/editions or only to some, or if there is no edition statement, give such a statement in the title and statement of responsibility area.

[1.2C2]

1.3. MATERIAL (OR TYPE OF PUBLICATION) SPECIFIC DETAILS AREA

This area is not defined for archival materials.

1.4. DATE AREA

This area is not defined for archival cataloging. Include the date, inclusive dates, or bulk dates of archival and manuscript material as part of area 1 (see 1.1B5).

1.5 PHYSICAL DESCRIPTION AREA

Contents:
1.5A   Preliminary rule
1.5B   Statement of extent
1.5C   Other physical details
1.5D   Dimensions

1.5A. Preliminary rule

1.5A1. Punctuation

For information on the use of spaces before and after prescribed punctuation, see 1.0C.

If this area is not given as a separate paragraph, precede it by a period, space, dash, space (. --).

Precede other physical details by a colon.
Precede the dimensions by a semicolon.

1.5B. Statement of extent

1.5B1. Collections of archival material. Give the primary statement of extent of archival material in terms of the number of linear or cubic feet (meters in Canada) occupied, or in terms of the exact or approximate number of items[8] (expressed as *items*, *volumes*, etc.). If the statement of extent for a collection is given in terms of one unit of measurement and additional information in terms of another unit of measurement is required or desirable, add this additional information in parentheses. Express fractions of linear or cubic feet (or meters) as decimals.

> 87 items (0.5 linear ft.)
>
> ca. 10,200 items (14.7 cubic ft.)
> *or*
> 14.7 cubic ft. (ca. 10,200 items)
>
> 128 linear ft.
>
> 40 cubic meters
>
> 6 v. (1.5 linear ft.)
>
> 12 linear ft. (36 boxes)

If a collection consists of more than one type of material and each is measured in a different way, give separate statements of extent.

> ca. 1500 items
> 2 microfilm reels
> (*The collection consists of ca. 1500 items* and *2 microfilm reels*)

Optionally, if separate statements of extent are given and it is desirable to associate each statement of extent with a specific type of material, give the type of material as an introductory word or phrase.

> Diaries: 17 v.
> Correspondence: 0.5 linear ft.
> Architectural drawings: 6 items

If the statement of extent is complex and potentially confusing, explain it in a note.

[Institutional practices vary considerably in expressing extent. What is important is not that all institutions use the same terms in this area, but that the terms chosen are internally consistent and clearly indicate to a potential user the size of the collection.]

1.5B2. Single manuscripts. Describe an individual letter, diary, journal, account book, scrapbook, letter book, literary manuscript, etc., as one item, volume, etc. When known,

---

8. Items are defined here as intellectual entities, e.g., a letter is one item, a 600-page manuscript is one item, 12 poems on 7 leaves is 12 items, etc.

add in parentheses the number of pages or leaves (whether numbered or not) with text on them or the number or approximate number of items in a volume.

> 1 item (47 p.)
>
> 1 v. (32 leaves)
>
> 1 v. (ca. 500 items)

1.5B3. Microform and other copies of archival material. If a repository holds both the original and microform or digitized copies of material (and is describing both in the same bibliographic record), the extent is expressed in two separate statements: the extent of the originals (as formulated under 1.5B1) and the extent of the copies (in number of microfilm reels, microfilm cassettes or cartridges, microfiches, aperture cards, microopaques, compact discs, etc., as appropriate).

> 450 items.
> 2 microfilm reels

Optionally (see also 1.5B1)

> Originals: 450 items
> Copies: 2 microfilm reels

Repositories holding only microform or digitized copies of original archival material held elsewhere should give as the chief statement of extent the number of microfilm reels, microfilm cassettes or cartridges, microfiches, aperture cards, microopaques, compact discs, etc., as appropriate. If the extent of the original material is known (i.e., the number of items, volumes, feet, etc.) give this information in a note (see 1.7B2).

> 123 microfilm reels
>
> 4 microfiches
>
> 1 microopaque

If microfilm is not on a reel, or if the material occupies only part of a reel along with other unrelated material, give the number of feet of microfilm occupied by the material being cataloged if it can be ascertained easily. Otherwise, indicate that the material occupies only part of a reel (e.g., *Forms part of a reel*, *Partial microfilm reel*, etc.). If desired, add the number of frames on a single microfiche in parentheses.

> 3 ft. of microfilm
>
> 1 microfilm reel (12 ft.)
>
> 1 microfiche (120 frames)
>
> Partial microfilm reel

1.5C. Other physical details

1.5C1. Give any other physical details that the repository considers important (e.g., type of paper, the presence of illustrations or maps, or the type of binding). If a microform is negative, give that information.

> 1 microfilm reel (220 frames) : negative

> 147 microfilm reels : negative
>
> 20 leaves : vellum
>
> 6 v. : ill.
>
> 1 v. : bound in vellum

1.5D. Dimensions. *Optionally,* supply the dimensions of items, volumes, or containers according to the following guidelines.

1.5D1. Collections of archival materials. If the size of the items, containers, or volumes given in the statement of extent is uniform, give that size in centimeters. If the size is not uniform, give the size of the largest item, and add "or smaller."[9] Give the size in terms of height. Add the width if it is either less than half the height, or greater than the height. If cubic measurement is needed, add the width and the depth.

> 6 v. ; 30 cm. [*Height*]
>
> 20 items ; 20 x 30 cm. [*Height x width*]
>
> 10 v. ; 28 cm. or smaller
>
> 12 linear ft. (28 boxes) ; 26 x 10 x 39 cm. [*Height x width x depth*]

1.5D2. Single manuscripts. Give the height of single unbound manuscripts in centimeters to the next whole centimeter up. Add the width if it is less than half the height or greater than the height. If the manuscript is kept folded, add the dimensions when folded.
[4.5D1]

> 1 item (6 p.) ; 24 cm. [*Height*]
>
> 1 item (7 p.) ; 24 x 30 cm. [*Height x width*]
>
> 1 item (12 leaves) ; 20 cm. folded to 10 x 12 cm.
>
> 1 item (1 leaf) : parchment ; 35 x 66 cm. folded to 10 x 19 cm.

Give the height of a bound volume or case in centimeters, to the next whole centimeter. Add the width if it is either less than half the height, or greater than the height.

> 1 v. (131 leaves in case) ; 26 cm.
>
> 1 item (70 p. in case) ; 20 x 24 cm.

1.5D3. Microforms. Give the size of microopaques and aperture cards as height *x* width in centimeters. If the dimensions of a microfiche are other than 10.5 *x* 14.8 cm., give the height *x* width in centimeters. See AACR 2 rule 11.5D3.

Give the width of a microfilm in millimeters. *Optionally,* give the width of a microfilm only if it is other than 35 mm.

> 20 aperture cards ; 9 x 19 cm.
>
> 30 microfiches ; 10 x 15 cm.

---

9. Do not confuse statements of extent with dimensions. The linear or cubic footage of a collection or records series is an expression of its overall extent. Dimensions relate only to the size of the containers in which the materials are stored.

110 microfilm cassettes : negative ; 16 mm.

1 microfilm reel (28 ft.) ; 16 mm.

1.6. SERIES AREA

This area currently is not defined for archival materials, because of possible confusion arising from archival use of the term "series" (see 1.0A) and common library usage.

1.7. NOTE AREA

Contents:
1.7A   Preliminary rule
1.7B   Notes

1.7A. Preliminary rule

1.7A1. Punctuation
If this area is not given as a separate paragraph, precede it by a period, space, dash, space (. --).

Separate introductory wording from the main content of a note by a colon and a space. (See bold note below.)

Separate distinct subelements of a note not governed by normal rules of narrative punctuation by a semicolon and a space.

1.7B. Notes. Make notes as set out in the following subrules.

[In formatting notes for USMARC catalog records, institutions will need to decide to what purposes the information in the notes ultimately will be put. For example, subelements of most note fields given below translate into equivalent USMARC subfields. If the intention is to sort on these subelements, the note will need to be structured to facilitate that sorting. If, on the other hand, the need is for an eye-readable narrative note, most content designation can be ignored.

In addition, catalogers need to be aware that there are certain print/display constants inherent in some USMARC fields that are implemented differently in different systems. Where prescribed or recommended introductory wording is generated by a given system implementation, such wording <u>should not</u> be incorporated in the cataloging itself.]

1.7B1. Biographical/Historical. Record briefly any significant information on the creator/author of the archival material required to make its nature or scope clear. For persons this may include place of birth and domicile, variant names, occupations (if relevant to the materials), and significant accomplishments (if reflected in the materials). Dates of birth and death may also be given here. For corporate bodies, this may include information on the functions, purpose, and history of the body, its administrative hierarchy, and earlier, variant, or successor names. This note may be divided into subelements consisting of a brief summary note and an expansion of the note.

Nurse and leader of the birth control movement.

Established in the War Department 3 Mar. 1865, to supervise all activities relating to refugees and freedmen and to assume custody of all abandoned or confiscated lands or property. Abolished 10 June 1872, and remaining functions transferred to the Freedman's Branch, Office of the Adjutant General and after 1879, to the Colored Troops Division of the Office of Adjutant General.

Historian, of Wilson, Raleigh, and Chapel Hill, N.C.; first archivist of the United States; secretary, North Carolina Historical Commission; professor at the University of North Carolina-Chapel Hill; and author.

[The purpose of this note is to establish an appropriate context by simply relating the creating entity to the described materials. Elaborate biographical or historical essays are usually not appropriate for a catalog record-- although complicated corporate archives may require rather more historical detail.]

1.7B2. Scope and content/Abstract. Give information relating to the general contents, nature, and scope of the described materials. For archival collections, give (in this order) the specific types and forms of material present, noting the presence of graphic or other nontextual materials such as illustrations, maps, charts, drawings, plans, photographs, sound recordings, or computer files; the dates within which the material bulks largest (if appropriate); when appropriate, the functions or activities resulting in the creation of the records; and the most significant topics, events, persons, places, etc., represented. For collections containing correspondence, if desired list or characterize the most significant correspondents. If desired, also give the inclusive dates and/or extent for each type of material or for subunits within a collection. This note may be divided into subelements consisting of a brief note and an expansion of the note.

For an individual manuscript, give the form of the item and, for a letter, the recipient (if this information is not already in the title statement). In addition, give the date of delivery of a speech, sermon, etc., if it differs from the date of the manuscript as given in the title. Finally, abstract the contents of the item, giving significant topics, persons, places, events, etc., mentioned or documented.

Correspondence, essays, and notebooks, covering the period when White was serving in the American embassy in Berlin. The papers relate chiefly to U.S. relations with Germany and the rise of Hitler and the Nazi Party, though there is some material relating to Greece in World War I. Correspondents include William E. Dodd, John G. Erhardt, George S. Messersmith, Jay Pierrepont Moffat, William Phillips, and Thomas M. Wilson.

Correspondence, diaries (1914-1953), articles, speeches, lectures, clippings, scrapbooks, printed matter, photographs, memorabilia, and organizational records relating to Mrs. Sanger's extensive activities on behalf of birth control in the U.S. and throughout the world. Includes material relating to many national and international congresses and conferences organized by Mrs. Sanger, her campaign to enlist public support for federal legislation on birth control, and material relating to her interest and activity in Socialist politics and liberal reform groups. Also included are records of various birth control groups with which she was associated, including the American Birth Control League, Birth Control Clinical Research Bureau, the National Committee on Federal Legislation for Birth Control, Birth Control Federation of America, Margaret Sanger Research Bureau, and the Planned Parenthood Federation of America. Correspondents include...

Records of Commissioner Oliver Otis Howard (1830-1909) and his adjutants, including annual and monthly reports from assistant commissioners, letter books, letters received and registers, endorsement books, and circulars and special orders issued. There are also station books of officers and civilians, appointment registers, and volumes of report synopses. Also includes records of the chief medical officer, 1865-1871, chief disbursing officer, 1865-1872, Land Division, 1865-1871, Claim Division, 1866-1872, Education Division, 1865-1871, chief quartermaster, 1866-1872, and Archives Division, 1869-1872. Most of these consist of reports, letters received and registers, letter books, endorsement books, and volumes of report synopses or registers of claimants compiled in the bureau. There are also records of Assistant Inspector General Whittlesey relating to distribution of supplies to the South, 1867-1868.

Holograph petition of Burns to James Monroe, secretary of state, to obtain a letter of marque and reprisal for the schooner Snap Dragon, New Bern, N.C.

The sound recordings date from 1938 to 1952. Several selections consist of political advertisements for the 1949 mayoral campaign. Others include a 1951 press conference with an assistant to Marcantonio, Clifford T. McAvoy, who was running for City Council; a political speech given by Marcantonio in 1938 to the Harlem Legislative Committee; a 1943 speech on the downfall of Mussolini; and a 1952 speech given to the American Labor Party.

Relates to supplies and uniforms for soldiers in the Continental Army.

Holograph journal and log kept by Brantz on a voyage (10 Mar.-10 Sept. 1793) aboard the brig Equality from Baltimore around the Cape of Good Hope to the Isle of France (i.e. Mauritius); journal and log of a voyage (11 Dec. 1793-27 Jan. 1794) aboard the ship Chase from the Isle of France to Ascension Island in the South Atlantic; and journal and log of a voyage (27 Jan.-14 July 1794) aboard the brig Equality from Ascension Island to Ostend and from Ostend to Baltimore. Includes meteorological and navigational information in addition to routines of shipboard life.

This series consists of computer (floppy disk) files relating to persons with expired/inactive social worker licenses. Each applicant's file records the name, last known address, license number, level of license, how licensed, and year initially licensed. An annual printout is generated.

This collection consists mainly of letters received by Mary Cox Collins; 274 of the letters are from her husband, with numerous letters from her children.

1.7B3. Linking entry complexity. Make a note concerning any complex hierarchical relationship between catalog records, i.e., when the material being described is a component part or subunit of another collection or series that is an existing bibliographic entity. Using appropriate introductory wording such as *Forms part of:* (normally used for subunits within larger groups) or *In:* (normally used for items within larger groups), give the title for the hierarchically superior unit as formulated under the principles outlined in 1.1A-1.1E.

> Forms part of: Naval Historical Foundation manuscript collection.

> Forms part of: War Department collection of Confederate records (Record Group 109).

> In: Oppenheimer, J. Robert, 1904-1967. Papers, 1927-1967.

1.7B4. Additional physical form available. When the repository has the original *and* a copy of all or part of the material being described, make a note to record information about the additional (i.e., different) physical format(s) in which the described material is available for use at the holding repository and/or in published form. If the latter, also record availability information (source, order number, condition, etc.). Add appropriate introductory wording to subelements when it is necessary to make the nature and intent of their information clear. See also 1.5B3 for recording extent of originals and copy.

> Diaries and correspondence available on microfilm for use in repository only.

> Also available on microfilm; source: Library of Congress Photoduplication Service, Washington, D.C. 20540; order no.: 18,447.

1.7B5. Reproduction. Record information that the material being described is a copy of originals that either are located elsewhere or have been destroyed. Record (in order and if available) the type of reproduction, the place of reproduction, the agency responsible for the reproduction, the date of the reproduction, a physical description of the reproduction, and a bibliographic series statement (if appropriate). If the originals have been destroyed after copying or are no longer extant, record this information. Add appropriate introductory wording to subelements when it is necessary to make the nature and intent of the information clear.

> In part, photocopies. Copied at: University of North Carolina at Chapel Hill, Southern Historical Collection; 1978.

> Photocopies (negative). Copied at: Archives Nationales, Paris, France; 1937.

> Microfilm; originals destroyed after filming.

> Microfilm. Filmed at: Duke University Library, Manuscript Department; filmed by: University Publications of America, Inc.; 1987; 5 microfilm reels (nos. 18-22); series statement: Records of ante-bellum southern plantations, series F, selections from the Manuscript Department, Duke University Library, part 1.

1.7B6. Location of originals/duplicates. Record the name and, *optionally*, the address of repositories, other than the cataloging repository, with custody of the originals or duplicate copies of the described material. Subelements may include the name of the custodian repository, its address, the country of the repository, and its telephone number. Begin the note with appropriate introductory wording (e.g., *Originals in:* or *Photocopies* or *Transcripts* or *Microfilm*, etc. *in:*).

> Originals in: Manuscripts and Archives, Yale University Library; Box 1603A Yale Station, New Haven, CT 06520.

Originals of diaries in: Manuscript Division, Library of Congress; Washington, D.C. 20540.

[The cataloging of microform and other copies of archival materials has always presented certain problems. With such copies running the gamut from highly individualized selections of material (often made for a specific patron) to full-blown scholarly editions prepared for publication often as part of a publication series (e.g., the Records of ante-bellum southern plantations **series illustration given above), the decision on whether and how to record "publication" details has often been difficult. Determinations on whether to catalog such microforms as publications or as archival material will depend on the purposes of the catalog and the needs of the repository for more or less detail and content analysis as part of the description. For those institutions wishing to catalog such material archivally, it is clear that the notes above can accommodate the publication details.**[10]

1.7B7. Organization and arrangement. Record information about the organization and arrangement of the materials being described. *Organization* relates to the manner in which the materials have been subdivided into smaller units, such as record groups divided into series and series into subseries. *Arrangement* relates to the pattern of arrangement (e.g., alphabetical, chronological, etc.) of materials within the unit described.

Organized into the following series: I. General correspondence, 1812-1868; II. William Q. Force papers, 1843-1944; III. Printer's file, 1818-1846; IV. Subject file, 1822-1864; V. Financial papers, 1816-1867; VI. Historical working papers, undated; VII. Transcripts, subseries A-E as follows: A. American Archives, 1774-1776; B. Printed sources, 1526-1850; C. Papers of the Continental Congress, 1770-1796; D. Papers of George Washington, 1775-1796; E. Manuscript sources; VIII. Manuscript collections, subseries A-E as follows: A. George Chalmers collection, 1641-1824; B. Hazard collection, 1170-1832; C. Hispanic collection, 1527-1811; D. Manuscripts from various sources, 1632-1873; IX. Historical manuscripts, 1501-1866; X. Force manuscripts in the collections of the Library of Congress, National Archives and Records Service, and the Maryland Hall of Records.

Arrangement: Chronological within record type (minutes, general memoranda, legislative memoranda, etc.) in each volume.

Diaries and notebooks arranged chronologically, 1846-1903; family correspondence arranged chronologically, 1789-1825; general correspondence, arranged chronologically, 1875-1910; speeches and writings arranged chronologically, 1875-1910, and alphabetically thereunder by title; subject files arranged alphabetically by type of material.

Arrangement: Pre-1837 records: Chronological by court term, then by defendant's county of residence.

---

10. For a fuller discussion of these issues, see Weber, Lisa B., "Describing Microforms and the MARC Format," *Archival Informatics Newsletter* 1 (Summer 1987): 9-13.

1.7B8. Language. Make a note concerning the language or languages of the materials being described, unless they are noted elsewhere or are apparent from other elements of the description. Also note any distinctive alphabets or symbol systems employed.

> In Swedish.

> In German Fraktur.

> Chiefly in Russian longhand.

> English with typewritten French translations.

1.7B9. Provenance. Make a note concerning the history of the custody of the materials being cataloged. Give information (including dates) on collation and on successive transfers of ownership and custody of the materials.

> Originally collected by George Madison and arranged by his nephew, John Ferris, after Madison's death. Purchased by Henry Kapper in 1878 who added to the collection with materials purchased at auctions in Philadelphia and Paris, 1878-1893.

> Family correspondence originally collected by Henry Fitzhugh, willed to his wife Sara Jackson Fitzhugh and given by her to her grandson Jonathan Irving Jackson, who collected some further information about his grandmother and the papers of their relatives and Cellarsville neighbors, the Arnold Fitzhughs, before donating the materials, along with his own papers as mayor of Cellarsville, to the Historical Society.

> The Department of Correction placed these records on loan with Syracuse University from 1960 to 1977.

1.7B10. Immediate source of acquisition. Make a note on the donor or source (i.e., the immediate prior custodian) of the material being cataloged and, if desired, give the source's address. Indicate the manner or method (e.g., gift, purchase, deposit, transfer, etc.) of the acquisition and the date of the acquisition. *Optionally*, add accession number(s), purchase price, the relation of the source to the material, and other relevant information. For materials acquired from multiple sources, make multiple notes, specifying, if desired, materials received in each acquisition. If the source is unknown, record that information.

> Gift of Worthington C. Ford, 1907.

> Source unknown.

> Purchase, 1978.

> Deposit, 1903. Converted to gift, 1948.

> Gift of Mrs. Richard's daughter, JoAnn C. Richard, 1968.

> Orderly books: Transfer; Pension Office; 1909.
> Letter books: Transfer; State Department; 1915.

[Institutional practices may vary in expressing--or even suppressing--this information in a publicly accessible catalog record. See also the note under 1.7B.]

1.7B11. Restrictions on access. Record information about any restrictions imposed on access to the materials. Make a note specifying the details of the restriction, including the date when it will be lifted. Additional information may be recorded regarding the jurisdiction (i.e., the person, institution, or position or function through which the terms governing access are imposed, enforced, and may be appealed), physical access provisions, authorized users (i.e., individuals or a class of users to whom the restrictions do not apply), or authorization (i.e., the source of the authority for the restriction). Alternately, simply indicate the fact of the restriction.

> Access restricted.

> Closed to investigators until 1999.

> Family correspondence closed until 2010 or until the death of the donor.

> Classified under national security provisions; Department of Defense; Title 50, Chapter 401, U.S.C.

1.7B12. Terms governing use and reproduction. Record information about terms governing the use of the materials after access has been provided. This includes, but is not limited to, copyrights, film rights, trade restrictions, etc., that restrict the right to reproduce, exhibit, fictionalize, quote, etc. If the literary rights in materials were dedicated or reserved under previous copyright law, record that information. If the materials were received after 31 December 1977, and if copyright interests have been dedicated or reserved under new copyright law (Title 17, U.S.C.), record that information. Additional information may be added relating to jurisdiction, authorization, or authorized users (see definitions under 1.7B11).

> Information on literary rights available in the repository.

> Literary rights of Carrie Chapman Catt have been dedicated to the public.

> Copyright interests have been reserved.

> Photocopying of diaries is prohibited.

1.7B13. Cumulative index/finding aids. Identify or note the presence of any existing administrative and intellectual controls over the described materials (e.g., registers, inventories, calendars, series descriptions, card catalogs, institutional guides, etc.). If desired, give information regarding the degree of administrative, bibliographic, or physical control reflected in the finding aid and any citations to published or unpublished finding aids.

> Finding aid in the repository; folder level control.

> Card index in the repository.

> Described in: Library of Congress, Manuscript Division. Naval Historical Foundation Manuscript Collection: A Catalog. Washington, D.C.: Library of Congress, 1974.

1.7B14. Citation. Record a brief bibliographic citation[11] or reference to publications (other than finding aids) in which abstracts, citations, descriptions, calendars, or indexes

---

11. Citations given in rules 1.7B13, 1.7B14, and 1.7B16 follow bibliographic forms recommended in the *Chicago Manual of Style*, 13th ed. (Chicago: University of Chicago Press, 1982). Repositories may wish to use other forms based on alternate recommendations in *Chicago Manual of Style* or in AACR 2 (e.g., rule 1.7A4).

of the described materials have appeared. Include journal articles describing portions of the materials and guides describing the collection in terms of a particular subject focus. Use appropriate introductory wording (e.g., *Described in:*, *Listed in:*) in order to clarify the nature of the citation. If desired, give information on the exact location within the source.

> Described in: Library of Congress Acquisitions: Manuscript Division, 1979. Washington, D.C.: Library of Congress, 1981.

> Listed in: Ricci. Census, vol. 1, p. 857, no. 4.

> Arctic field notebooks cited in: Day, Harold. "Statistical Methods for Population Transport Estimation." Journal of Ecological Studies 7 (1974): 187.

1.7B15. Preferred citation of described materials. Record the format for the citation of the described material that is preferred by the custodian. Use the introductory phrase *Cite as:* to introduce the citation form.

> Cite as: James Hazen Hyde Papers, 1891-1941, New-York Historical Society.

> Cite as: Socialist Party of America Records, Manuscript Department, Duke University Library.

1.7B16. Publications. Record a citation to or information about a publication that is based on the use, study, or analysis of the described materials (e.g., historical studies, biographies, statistical reports). Citations or references to publications in which the materials have been cited, described, indexed, etc., are recorded in the citation note (see 1.7B14). If necessary, use appropriate introductory wording (e.g., *Publications:*, *Portions published in:*) in order to clarify the nature of the citation.

> Publications: Levine, Lawrence W. "William Shakespeare and the American People: A Study in Cultural Transformation." American Historical Review 89 (February 1984).

> Publications: Poetry: A Magazine of Verse 59 (1942): 295-308.

> Photographs published in: Mirer, Emma. Faces of Political Women. Boston: Whitehurst Press, 1984.

1.7B17. General note. Record any other descriptive information considered important but not falling within the definitions of the other notes. This may include information on physical details not given elsewhere, source of title, and title variations.

> Ms. torn in half and rejoined.

> Text heavily foxed.

> Incoming correspondence, 1855-1875, heavily damaged by rodent and insect infestation.

> Title transcribed from spine.

> Also known as: Anglo-Dutch War collection.

> Tape reels transferred from original acetate discs.

PART II

HEADINGS AND UNIFORM TITLES

Introduction

The basic premise underlying the interpretations offered in the chapters in Part II is that, whatever the differences that may exist between the bibliographic description of archival and other library material, there are nevertheless essential similarities. The most important similarity is to be found in the various headings or access points under which the descriptions are entered and/or found. The entire premise of bibliographic integration, in fact, rests upon the foundation of common and uniform headings among all bibliographic formats.

Chapters 21-25 of AACR 2 contain rules relating to choice and form of access points (headings) under which all bibliographic descriptions are entered in an integrated catalog. Because these headings must be constructed uniformly so that searches under a specific heading will yield all records regardless of format, no special provisions were made in these chapters for different headings for different bibliographic formats.

Traditionally, it has been these particular chapters that have presented the most problems for catalogers of archival material. Although this was originally because these chapters lacked any specificity regarding archival applications (particularly chapter 21), there was also the perception that the rules in chapters 22-25 were occasionally inconsistent with common archival wisdom and practice. Ultimately, however, the arguments and interests of bibliographic integration have been sufficiently compelling to overcome most of these difficulties.

However, the rules for determining the *choice* of access points (headings) as laid down in chapter 21 of AACR 2 have presented special problems. While it may be relatively easy for catalogers of archival material to understand the fact that no special provisions can be made for *forming* the various headings under which their descriptions are entered, it is considerably more difficult to understand and apply book-oriented prescriptions for *choosing* those headings.

Normally, the heading chosen for the main entry of a bibliographic description is a direct reflection of the entity (personal or corporate) chiefly responsible for the creation of the intellectual or artistic content of a work. Such distinctions are not easily made with archival material, however, since it is the provenance of the material that determines its content more than any bibliographic notions of responsibility. Consequently, the rules in chapter 21 have required substantial interpretation and expansion, so that archival catalogers may more clearly understand the principles and procedures involved in choosing appropriate headings for their bibliographic descriptions.

Some of the personal and corporate name headings that catalogers of archival material will need to use will be found in the Library of Congress Name Authority File (LCNAF), which is available online in both RLIN and OCLC and in microfiche from the Cataloging Distribution Service of the Library of Congress. These headings, which have been formed according to the appropriate AACR 2 rules and rule interpretations, should be used for all bibliographic records, regardless of the format of the material being cataloged.

However, many of the headings in this file were created for persons or corporate bodies that had *published* something or that were sufficiently prominent to have had something published *about* them. This is not true of many individuals and corporate bodies represented in archival collections, so headings for them may never have been established in the authority files. If the heading for a person or corporate body is not found in the LCNAF, formulate it according to the rules in chapters 3-5 (resolving any problems or questions, of course, by resorting to chapters 22-25 of AACR 2).

REFERENCES

Some of the rules in the chapters on forming headings carry instructions on creating references from forms of headings not used or variant headings (*see* references, usually denoted by an *x* preceding them). These references are never actually part of any specific bibliographic record, but are instead intended for use in authority records. Consequently, the instructions on making these references are specifically intended for catalogers creating authority records, either in making and maintaining a local authority file or in constructing authority records for the LCNAF. Although this manual is not designed to provide specific guidelines for the construction of authority files, some of these instructions nevertheless have been retained to illustrate the principles expounded in the various rules. For additional information on references, see chapter 26 of AACR 2.

FORM OF EXAMPLES

Examples are given to illustrate individual rules. The construction of a complete heading often requires several rules. Therefore, the form of a name shown in an example does not necessarily correspond to the complete and authorized heading that one might find for that name in the Library of Congress Name Authority File. In other words, *do not use the examples given in this manual as headings in bibliographic records without checking the authority file*.

CHAPTER 2

CHOICE OF ACCESS POINTS

Contents

Added Entries

2.0. INTRODUCTORY RULES

2.0A. Main and added entries

The rules in this chapter are rules for determining the choice of access points (headings) under which a bibliographic description (see Part I) is entered in a catalog. The rules give instructions on the choice of one of these access points as the main entry heading, the others being added entry headings.

In general, each rule only gives instructions on those access points that are explicitly covered by the rule. Certain general points are dealt with in the rules on added entries (see 2.2-2.3).

2.0B. Sources for determining access points

Generally, determine access points for the material being cataloged from its chief source of information (see 1.0B1). When statements appearing in the chief source are ambiguous or insufficient, use information appearing outside the material and the chief source for determining access points. However, all access points should be justified in the catalog record.

2.0C. Forms of examples

The examples, in general, follow ISBD conventions (including ISBD punctuation). However, in some cases a transcription of the data is given without those conventions and punctuation. In particular, some of the names of persons or corporate bodies and other data occurring before the title proper are given first followed by a period.

2.0D. Designations of function

Optionally, in the cases noted below, add an abbreviated designation of function to a heading for a person.

FUNCTION PERFORMED	DESIGNATION
compiler	*comp.*
editor	*ed.*
illustrator	*ill.*
translator	tr.

Add other designations to headings as instructed in particular rules.

In specialist and archival cataloging, when desirable for identification or file arrangement, add designations from standard lists appropriate to the material being cataloged.[1]

[Two common designations or "relator terms" used in archival cataloging include *collector* **for the person principally responsible for assembling an artificial collection (see 2.1A4), and** *interviewee* **used for the subject of an oral history interview entered as a main or secondary entry (see 2.1A6). These terms are not abbreviated.]**

2.1. BASIC RULE

Enter a body of archival materials, on the basis of provenance, under the name of the person, family, or corporate body chiefly responsible for its creation.

---

1. See, for example, "Relator Terms for Rare Book, Manuscript, and Special Collections Cataloging, 3rd ed." *College and Research Libraries News* 48 (Oct. 1987): 553-557.

Archival materials are normally formed around or emanate from a person, family group, or corporate body. The responsibility for the intellectual content of these materials is directly related to archival principles of provenance rather than to the more deliberate creative relationship existing between books and their authors. For example, the papers of an individual, even though they may actually contain items written by other individuals, are nevertheless a reflection of that person's life and activities. As such, these papers in their totality may be said to have been "created" by the person.

Similarly, corporate archives and government records series may be said to be "works" of information brought together by a body for a specified purpose or in the course of fulfilling a function. Even though there may be documents or information within these records that technically were created by another individual, group, or agency, primary responsibility for the totality of the intellectual content of these records rests with the agency that created the series by collecting the information and maintaining it over time.

Thus, the assignment of main entries for archival materials on the basis of their provenance is consistent with the general principles given in AACR 2 of entry under the entity chiefly responsible for the creation of a work.

Apply the following rules in determining choice of heading for a bibliographic description of a hierarchically subordinate unit of a larger entity (e.g., item, folder, or series level descriptions of archival materials also described at the collection level). All bibliographic descriptions should be entered under the heading most appropriate for the material being described. Thus, a subordinate unit may be entered under a different heading from its hierarchically superior unit.

2.1A. Entry under personal name

2.1A1. Personal papers of an individual. Enter a body of archival materials of an individual person under the appropriate heading for that person. Personal papers may consist of manuscript material, papers, and other material by and/or to a given person. For example, a collection of papers consisting of incoming letters to an individual from a variety of persons and copies of outgoing letters from that individual, along with drafts of writings by and other materials obviously accumulated by that individual, would be entered under the heading for that person.

> **Hamilton, Alexander**, 1757-1804.
> Papers, 1703-1908.

> **Bissell, Kenneth McLeod**, 1884-1972.
> Four years at Yale : diaries, 1903 Sept. 16-1907 Oct. 5.

Exception: An individual letter or collection of letters not sufficiently identified as the "papers" of the recipient(s) may be entered under the heading for the author (see 2.1A5).

2.1A2. Personal papers of two or more individuals. If a collection of archival material consists of papers and other material of two or more persons and the integrity of its provenance generally appears to be intact, enter the material under the heading for either the more prominent person (based upon reference sources) or the person whose papers predominate. If no individual predominates or can be considered more prominent make the main entry under title (see 2.1C2-2.1C3) and make added entries for all persons (see 2.3A).

> **Flanner, Janet**, 1892- [*Main entry*]
> Janet Flanner-Solita Solano papers, 1870-1975.
> [*Added entry under the heading for Solita Solano*]

> **Dumont, Henry**, 1878-1949. [*Main entry*]
> Henry and Nina Webster Dumont papers, 1905-1936.
> [*Added entry under heading for Nina Webster Dumont*]

2.1A3. Family papers. If a collection of archival materials has been formed around or generated by several generations of, or a number of individuals in, the same family, enter it under the heading for the family name. If one individual is the principal focus of the family archives, enter them under the heading for the individual and use the title *Family papers*. If the material consists of the papers of two or more families, enter them under title (see 2.1C5).

> **Schramm family**.
> Papers, 1932-1971.

> **Richardson, James Burchell.**
> Family papers, 1803-1910.

2.1A4. Artificial collections. A collection of archival material that has been artificially accumulated around a person, subject, event, activity, etc., without regard to the archival integrity or provenance of the materials is entered under the heading for the person chiefly responsible for the creation of the collection as such. Add the term *collector* to the heading. If the collector is unknown, enter the collection under title. If the collection is already known under another title, enter it under that title. If there is no title, supply a title reflecting the nature and/or focus of the collection.

> **Porter, John K. (John Kilham)**, 1819-1892, *collector*.
> John K. Porter autograph collection, 1600-1882.

> **Purland, Theodosius**, *collector*.
> Collection of papers on mesmerism, 1842-1854.

> **Morgan, J. Pierpont (John Pierpont)**, 1837-1913, *collector*.
> The John Pierpont Morgan collection of the signers of the Declaration of Independence, 1761-1803.

2.1A5. Entry under author. Enter an individual manuscript, letter, diary, etc., of known authorship or origin under the heading for the person chiefly responsible for the intellectual content of the item. Enter a handwritten or typescript copy of an item under its original author (make an added entry for the copyist, see 2.3A3). Enter a manuscript letter, document, etc., under the heading for the author or signer of the item (whether or not the text is in that person's hand). Enter a collection of letters, documents, manuscripts, etc., written or signed by the same person under the heading for that person.

> **Styron, William**, 1925-
> Sophie's choice : holograph / by William Styron.

> **Burns, Otway**, 1775-1850.
> Petition : to James Monroe, 1813 July 1.

> **Washington, Bushrod**, 1762-1829.
> ALS : to Henry Lee, 1810 Sept. 12.

> **Morse, Samuel Finley Breese**, 1791-1872.
> Letters : to Mrs. Silliman, 1845 Jan. 1-Oct. 13.

2.1A6. Oral history interviews/collections. Enter an individual oral history interview (whether on audio or video tape or in typed transcription) under the heading for the person interviewed. Follow the heading with the relator term *interviewee*. Make added entries for the interviewers, as appropriate. For collections of oral history material relating to diverse topics and individuals, follow the appropriate guidelines for choosing headings (personal or corporate) for collections. See also chapter 1 for guidelines for formulating titles of such collections.

> **Wiesel, Elie,** 1928- *interviewee.*
> Typed transcript of oral history interview, Duke University, Durham, N.C., 1987 Nov. 10.

> **Duke University. Living History Program.**
> Oral history collection, 1968-1988.

2.1B. **Entry under corporate name**

2.1B1. Definition. A corporate body is an organization or a group of persons that is identified by a particular name and that acts, or may act, as an entity. Consider a corporate body to have a name if the words referring to it are a specific appellation rather than a general description. Consider a body to have a name if, in a script and language using capital letters for proper names, the initial letters of the words referring to a corporate body are consistently capitalized, and/or if, in a language using articles, the words are always associated with a definite article. Typical examples of corporate bodies are associations, institutions, business firms, nonprofit enterprises, governments, government agencies, projects and programs, religious bodies, local churches, and conferences.[2]

Some corporate bodies are subordinate to other bodies (e.g., the Peabody Museum of Natural History is subordinate to Yale University; the Annual General Meeting is subordinate to the Canadian Library Association).

Consider ad hoc events (such as athletic contests, exhibitions, expeditions, fairs, and festivals) and vessels (e.g., ships and spacecraft) to be corporate bodies.

[21.1B1]

2.1B2. General rule

Enter the records of a corporate body under the appropriate heading for that body. Records consist of any documentation created in the course of fulfilling the purposes and functions of the corporate body, and may include such materials as correspondence,

---

2. Conferences are meetings of individuals or representatives of various bodies for the purpose of discussing and acting on topics of common interest, or meetings of representatives of a corporate body that constitute its legislative or governing body. Conferences include any named meeting that is entered directly under its own name and any named meeting that is entered subordinately to a heading for a corporate body.

minutes, legal and financial records, account books, log books, computer files, photographs, motion pictures, videorecordings, etc.

The heading chosen should accurately reflect the administrative unit having most direct responsibility for the creation and provenance of the materials described. Thus, if materials are being described at the record series level, the description will be entered under the heading for the agency that either created or maintained the series as a discrete entity.

> **Bollingen Foundation**.
> Records, 1939-1973.

> **Auburn University. Division of Student Services**.
> Dean of Student Service records, 1965-1980.

> **United States. Bureau of Insular Affairs**.
> Records, 1868-1945.

2.1B3. Corporate body/agency name change. When a corporate body or agency name has changed over the period of time covered by the records or series, enter the description under the heading for the last name represented in the materials. If records are subsequently added reflecting a later name change, change the heading to correspond to that name. Make an added name-title entry under the heading for each predecessor agency name represented in the collection (see 2.3D).

> **New York (State). Dept. of Social Services**.
> Reports of poorhouses, 1876-1940.
> (*Added entries for State Board of Charities, 1876-1910 and Department of Mental Hygiene, 1910-1920*)
>
> New York (State). State Board of Charities. Reports of poorhouses, 1876-1910.
> New York (State). Dept. of Mental Hygiene. Reports of poorhouses, 1910-1920.

2.1B4. Agency transfer of records. If an agency has had legal or physical custody of a record series, but was not responsible for creating a series or for continuing and maintaining the series, enter under the name of the agency that created the series.

2.1B5. Individual official or government documents. Enter an individual official document (e.g., indenture, deed, contract, etc.) under the heading for the corporate body having direct responsibility for administering the function reflected in the document. If the body is not specifically identified or its identity is not clear, enter the document under the heading for the government jurisdiction (e.g., state, county, etc.) named in the document. If the jurisdiction is not clear or known, enter the document under the name of the office of the principal signer. Make added entries for all significant signers.

> **Wake County (N.C.)**
> Land indenture, 1845 Oct. 15.

> **Burlington (Wis.). Mayor**.
> May Day proclamation, 1959 May 1.

2.1C. Entry under title

2.1C1. General rule. When the author or creator is unknown, or in cases of indistinct, unknown, or mixed provenance and origin, enter archival materials directly under title according to the following rules.

2.1C2. Artificial collections. Enter under title collections that have been collected or assembled by an individual but that are known under another name or title. Make an added entry for the collector when known (see 2.3C).

> **Harkness collection**, 1525-1651.
>
> **Shaker collection**, 1792-1937.

2.1C3. Personal papers of two or more individuals. Enter under title a collection of the personal papers of two or more individuals where no one person can be identified as more prominent or predominating and where the individuals are not members of the same family (see 2.1A2). Make added entries for the principal persons represented in the papers or for those persons named in the title (see 2.3A).

> **Ebenezer Sprout-William Shepard orderly book,** 1779-1780.
> *(Make added entries under headings for Sprout and Shepard)*

2.1C4. Nonarchival corporate collections. Enter under title archival materials collected by a corporate body that are not archival records of that body, i.e., not generated by that body's administrative or organizational activities. If the corporate collector is not the same as the repository holding the collection, make an added entry for it (see 2.3E).

> **Forest History Society oral history interviews,** 1957-1960.
> *(Oral history interviews with persons involved in logging and lumbering, conducted for the Forest History Society; not administrative or organizational records of the Forest History Society)*

2.1C5. Multiple family papers. Enter under title the combined papers of two or more families (see 2.1A3). Make an added entry for each of the families named in the title (see 2.3B).

> **Short-Harrison-Symmes family papers,** 1760-1878.
> *(Make added entries under headings for Short family, Harrison family, Symmes family)*

2.1C6. Manuscripts and collections of manuscripts of unknown origin or authorship. Enter under title (either formal title or supplied title based on subject, form, or content) manuscripts and manuscript collections for which the author or creator is unknown.

> **Analecta anglicana** : commonplace books.
>
> **New Bern Civil War collection.**

Added Entries

2.2. GENERAL RULE

2.2A. Make added entries to provide access to bibliographic descriptions in addition to the access provided by the main entry heading.

[21.29A]

2.2B. In addition, make added entries under other headings for persons and corporate bodies and under titles as instructed in 2.3.

[21.29B]

2.2C. Make an added entry under the heading for a person or a corporate body or under a title if some catalog users might suppose that the description of the material/item would be found under that heading or title rather than under the heading or title chosen for the main entry.

[21.29C]

2.2D. If, in the context of a given catalog, an added entry is required under a heading or title other than those prescribed in 2.3, make it.

[21.29D]

2.2E. Construct a heading for an added entry according to the instructions in chapters 3-6 (AACR 2 chapters 22-25). For instructions on the construction of name-title added entries, see 2.3G.

[21.29E]

2.2F. If the reason for an added entry is not apparent from the title or statement of responsibility, be certain that the name of the person or body or the title in the added entry is given in a note.

[21.29F]

2.3. SPECIFIC RULES

2.3A. Two or more persons or corporate bodies involved

2.3A1. If the main entry for a collection of papers of two or more individuals is under the heading for the more prominent or predominant person, make added entries under the headings for the other persons.

2.3A2. If the statement of responsibility for an individual manuscript reflects a joint-author relationship, make an added entry under the heading(s) for the person(s) not given in the main entry.

2.3A3. If a manuscript copy of an item is entered under the heading for the author of that item, make an added entry under the heading for the person in whose hand the copy was made.

2.3A4. If a collection of family papers is entered under the heading for the person most prominently represented in the papers, make an added entry under the heading for the family name and under the heading for the name of any other family member substantially represented.

2.3B. Multiple family papers. If the papers of two or more families have been entered under title, make an added entry under the heading for each individual family name.

2.3C. Collections. If a group of archival materials that have been collected by an individual, but that are better known by another name are entered under that name as title, make an added entry under the heading for the collector.

2.3D. Predecessor corporate bodies. When a group of government or corporate records reflecting corporate body/agency name changes over time is entered under the heading for the latest name represented, make an added entry under the heading for each previous name represented in the material described.

2.3E. Nonarchival corporate collections. If a manuscript collection or record series that is in the custody of a corporate body is not archival records of that body and is entered under title (see 2.1C4), make an added entry under the heading for the corporate collector. *Optionally*, if the collection was created by the repository holding the collection, do not make an added entry under the heading for the repository.

2.3F. Papers or records of one entity within the papers or records of another entity. When the papers of an individual, group of individuals, family, etc., or the records of a corporate body contain within them the papers of another individual or family, or records of another body to a degree insufficient to be reflected in the title but nevertheless significant enough to form a discrete unit or series within the larger collection, make a name-title added entry for the papers or records.

> **Force, William Q. Papers, 1843-1944.**
> *(A series within the collection cataloged as the Peter Force papers)*

> **College of Saint Paul. Financial records, 1858 Jan. 1-1861 Dec. 31.**
> *(In the collection cataloged as the Edward D. Neill papers)*

> **Margaret Sanger Research Bureau. Records, 1924-1953.**
> *(In the collection cataloged as the Margaret Sanger papers)*

2.3G. Titles. If a collection of archival material contains a single manuscript or any other significant bibliographic entity (e.g., film, sound recording, graphic, etc.) to which the cataloging agency wants to provide access, make an added entry (name-title or title, as appropriate) under the heading for the item. An added entry for a bibliographic entity is constructed in the same manner as it would be if entered on its own (e.g., main entry, if applicable, and title).

> **Neill, Edward D. (Edward Duffield), 1823-1893. Early French posts in Minnesota, 186-?**
> *(Single manuscript within the collection cataloged as the Edward D. Neill papers)*

> **Gotcha! (Motion picture)**
> *(A copy of the motion picture included within a collection)*

CHAPTER 3

HEADINGS FOR PERSONS

Contents

Choice of Name

Entry Element

Additions to Names

Choice of Name

3.1. GENERAL RULE

3.1A. Choose, as the basis of the heading for a person, the name by which he or she is commonly known. This may be the person's real name, pseudonym, title of nobility, nickname, initials, or other appellation. Treat a roman numeral associated with a given name (as, for example, in the case of some popes, royalty, and ecclesiastics) as part of the name. For the treatment of the names of authors using one or more pseudonyms or a real name and one or more pseudonyms, see 3.2B. For the form of the name used in headings, see 3.4-3.13.

[22.1A]

| | **D. W. Griffith** |
| *not* | David Wark Griffith |

| | **Jimmy Carter** |
| *not* | James Earl Carter |

| | **H. D.** |
| *not* | Hilda Doolittle |

Queen Elizabeth II

Pope John Paul II

3.1B. Determine the name by which a person is commonly known from the chief sources of information (see 1.0B1) and/or from reference sources issued in his or her language or country of residence or activity.[1]

[22.1B]

Spacing and punctuation conventions for personal name headings established subsequent to AACR 2 through Library of Congress rule interpretations have been adopted in the examples in this chapter.

---

1. In addition to standard biographical reference works such as *Who Was Who in America*, the *Dictionary of American Biography*, *Webster's Biographical Dictionary*, the *Dictionary of American History*, and *Current Biography*, reference sources may also include books, articles, and manuscript materials written about a person.

3.1C. Include any titles of nobility or terms of honor (see also 3.10) or words or phrases (see also 3.7 and 3.12) that commonly appear in association with the name either wholly or in part. For the treatment of other terms appearing in association with the name, see 3.16B.

[22.1C]

> **Sir Richard Acland**
>
> **Duke of Wellington**
>
> **Viscountess Astor**
>
> **Sister Mary Joseph**

3.1D. Diacritical marks and hyphens

3.1D1. Accents, etc. Include accents and other diacritical marks appearing in a name. Supply them if it is certain that they are integral to a name but have been omitted in the source(s) from which the name is taken.

[22.1D1]

> **Jacques Lefèvre d'Étaples**
>
> **Éliphas Lévi**
> (*Sometimes appears without diacritical marks*)

3.1D2. Hyphens. Retain hyphens between given names if they are used by the bearer of the name.

[22.1D2]

> **Gian-Carlo Menotti**
>
> **Jean-Léon Jaurès**

Include hyphens in romanized names if they are prescribed by the romanization system adopted by the cataloging agency.

> **Jung-lu**
>
> **Li Fei-kan**

Omit a hyphen that joins one of a person's forenames to the surname.

> **Lucien Graux**
> (*Name appears as* Lucien-Graux)

3.2. CHOICE AMONG DIFFERENT NAMES

3.2A. Predominant name

If a person (other than one using a pseudonym or pseudonyms) is known by more than one name, choose the name by which the person is clearly most commonly known, if there is one. Otherwise, choose one name or form of name according to the following order of preference:

[22.2A]

> a) the name that appears most frequently in the person's published works (if any)

b) the name the appears most frequently in the archival materials being described

c) the name that appears most frequently in reference sources

d) the latest name.

If a person's name shows a nickname in quotation marks or within parentheses as a part of other forename(s), omit the nickname in formulating the heading.

[RI]

> Name used: Martin (Bud) Schulman
> Heading: **Schulman, Martin**

If a married woman's name shows her own forenames in parentheses as part of her married name, omit the parenthesized elements in formulating the heading.

[RI]

> Name used: Mrs. John A. (Edna I.) Spies
> Heading: **Spies, John A., Mrs.**

3.2B. Pseudonyms

Because pseudonyms are, by definition, fictitious names assumed by authors, apply the following principles only to those persons primarily known as authors. For all other archival cataloging, choose personal name headings according to other relevant rules in this chapter, preferring, whenever possible, a person's real and full name to any nicknames, pseudonyms, pet names, etc., unless indications of usage dictate otherwise (see also 3.3A).

3.2B1. One pseudonym.
If all the works by one person appear under one pseudonym, choose the pseudonym. If the real name is known, make a reference from the real name to the pseudonym.

[22.2B1]

> **Yukio Mishima**
> *not*   Kimitake Hiraoka
>
> **George Orwell**
> *not*   Eric Arthur Blair
>
> **Woody Allen**
> *not*   Allen Stewart Konigsberg

3.2B2. Separate bibliographic identities.
If a person has established two or more bibliographic identities, as indicated by the fact that works of one type appear under one pseudonym and works of other types appear under other pseudonyms or the person's real name, choose, as the basis for the heading for each group of works, the name by which works in that group are identified. Make references to connect the names. In case of doubt, do not consider a person to have separate bibliographic identities.

[22.2B2]

> **[For archival cataloging of the personal papers of a person known generally under a literary pseudonym, choose the person's real name, assuming that the papers constitute a different bibliographic identity from any published works appearing under one or more pseudonyms. The authority record for such a person will carry** *see also* **references to all other names and pseudonyms.]**

J.I.M. Stewart
(*Real name used in "serious" novels and critical works*)
Michael Innes
(*Pseudonym used in detective novels*)

C. Day-Lewis
(*Real name used in poetic and critical works*)
Nicholas Blake
(*Pseudonym used in detective novels*)

Charles L. Dodgson
(*Real name used in works on mathematics and logic*)
Lewis Carroll
(*Pseudonym used in literary works*)

Frederic Dannay
(*Real name used in his personal papers*)
Ellery Queen
(*Shared pseudonym used in detective novels with Manfred Lee; see also AACR 2 rule 21.6D*)

3.2B3. Contemporary authors. If a contemporary author uses more than one pseudonym or his or her real name and one or more pseudonyms, use, as the basis for the heading for each work, the name appearing in it. Make references to connect the names.

[22.2B3]

Ed McBain
Evan Hunter
(*Pseudonyms used by the same person*)

Philippa Carr
Victoria Holt
Kathleen Kellow
Jean Plaidy
Ellalice Tate
(*Pseudonyms used by the same person*)

Kingsley Amis
(*Real name used in most works*)
Robert Markham
(*Pseudonym used in one work*)

If, in the works of contemporary authors, different names appear in different editions of the same work or two or more names appear in one edition, choose, for all editions, the name most frequently used in editions of the work. If that cannot be determined readily, choose the name appearing in the latest available edition of the work. Make name-title references from the other name or names.

3.2B4. If a person using more than one pseudonym or his or her real name and one or more pseudonyms

neither   has established separate bibliographic identities (see 3.2B2)
nor   is a contemporary author (see see 3.2B3)

51

choose, as the basis for the heading, the name by which that person has come to be identified in later editions of his or her works, in critical works, or in other reference sources[2] (in that order of preference). Make references from other names.

[22.2B4]

3.2C. Change of name

3.2C1. If a person (other than one using a pseudonym or pseudonyms) has changed his or her name, choose the latest name or form of name unless there is reason to believe that an earlier name will persist as the name by which the person is better known. Follow the same rule for a person who has acquired and become known by a title of nobility.

[22.2C1]

> **Dorothy Belle Hughes**
> *not* Dorothy Belle Flanagan
> *(Name used in published works before author's marriage)*

> **Jacqueline Onassis**
> *not* Jacqueline Bouvier
> *not* Jacqueline Kennedy
> *(Names used previously before marriage and during first marriage)*

> **Judy Garland**
> *not* Frances Gumm
> *(Stage name adopted, by which she is commonly known)*

> **Ford Madox Ford**
> *not* Ford Madox Hueffer
> *(Name changed from* Hueffer *to* Ford*)*

> **Muhammad Ali**
> *not* Cassius Clay
> *(Name changed from* Cassius Clay *to* Muhammad Ali*)*

> *but*

> **Benjamin Disraeli**
> *not* Earl of Beaconsfield
> *(Title acquired late in life; better known by earlier name)*

3.3. CHOICE AMONG DIFFERENT FORMS OF THE SAME NAME

3.3A. Fullness

3.3A1. If the forms of a name vary in fullness, choose the form most commonly found. As required, make references from the other form(s).

[22.3A1]

[For most individuals represented in archival collections who are not known primarily as authors, prefer the form whose usage appears to be

---

2. Disregard reference sources that always enter persons under their real names.

most common or that is most commonly found in reference sources.[3] **If no form seems to predominate, prefer the fuller or fullest form of the person's name.]**

> **Morris West**
> (*Most common form*: Morris West)
> (*Occasional form*: Morris L. West)

> **P. X. Smith**
> (*Most common form*: P. X. Smith)
> (*Occasional forms*: Peter Xavier Smith; Peter X. Smith; Xavier Smith)

If no one form predominates, choose the latest form. In case of doubt about which is the latest form, choose the fuller or fullest form.

Entry Element

3.4. GENERAL RULE

3.4A. If a person's name (chosen according to 3.1-3.3) consists of several parts, select as the entry element that part of the name under which the person would normally be listed in authoritative alphabetic lists[4] in his or her language or country of residence or activity. In applying this general rule, follow the instructions in 3.5-3.8. If, however, a person's preference is known to be different from the normal usage, follow that preference in selecting the entry element.

[22.4A]

3.4B. Order of elements

3.4B1. If the entry element is the first element of the name, enter the name in direct order.

[22.4B1]

> **Ram Gopal**

3.4B2. If the first element is a surname, follow it by a comma.

[22.4B2]

> **Chiang, Kai-shek**
> (*Name*: Chiang Kai-shek)
> (*Surname*: Chiang)

3.4B3. If the entry element is not the first element of the name, transpose the elements of the name preceding the entry element. Follow the entry element by a comma.

[22.4B3]

> **Cassatt, Mary**
> (*Name*: Mary Cassatt)

3.4B4. If the entry element is the proper name in a title of nobility (see 3.6), follow it by the personal name in direct order and then by the part of the title denoting rank. Precede the personal name and the part of the title denoting rank by commas.

[22.4B4]

---

3. Disregard reference sources that always enter persons under their full names.

4. Authoritative alphabetic lists means publications of the "who's who" type, not telephone directories or similar compilations.

Leighton, Frederick Leighton, *Baron*

Caradon, Hugh Foot, *Baron*

3.5. ENTRY UNDER SURNAME

3.5A. General rule

Enter a name containing a surname (or consisting only of a surname) under that surname (see also 3.12) unless subsequent rules (e.g., 3.6, 3.8) provide for entry under a different element.

[22.5A1]

Bernhardt, Sarah

Fitzgerald, Ella

Ching, Francis K. W.

If the surname is represented by an initial, but at least one element of the name is given in full, enter under the initial that represents the surname.

Q., Mike

3.5B. Element other than the first treated as a surname

If the name does not contain a surname but contains an element that identifies the individual and functions as a surname, enter under this element followed by a comma and the rest of the name.

[22.5B1]

Hus, Jan

Ali, Muhammad
   (*The American boxer*)

X, Malcolm

3.5C. Compound surnames

3.5C1. Preliminary rule. The following rules deal with the entry of surnames consisting of two of more proper names (referred to as "compound surnames") and names that may or may not contain compound surnames. Apply the rules in the order given. Refer from elements of compound surnames not chosen as the entry element.

[22.5C1]

3.5C2. Preferred or established form known. Enter a name containing a compound surname under the element by which the person prefers to be entered.[5] If this is unknown,

---

5. Take regular or occasional initializing of an element preceding a surname as an indication that that element is not used as part of the surname.

   Chavarri, Eduardo López
      (*Name sometimes appears as*: Eduardo L. Chavarri)

   Szentpál, Mária Sz.
      (*Name appears as*: Sz. Szentpál Mária)
      (*Husband's surname*: Szilági)

   Campbell, Julia Morrila de
      (*Name sometimes appears as: Julia M. de Campbell*)

enter the name under the element under which it is listed in reference sources[6] in the person's language or country of residence or activity.

[22.5C2]

> **Lloyd George, David**
> (*Paternal surname:* George)

> **Fénelon, François de Salignac de la Mothe-**

> **Machado de Assis, Joaquim Maria**
> (*Paternal surname:* de Assis)

3.5C3. Hyphenated surnames. If the elements of a compound surname are regularly or occasionally hyphenated, enter under the first element.

[22.5C3]

> **Day-Lewis, Cecil**

> **Henry-Bordeaux, Paule**

3.5C4. Other compound surnames, except those of married women whose surname consists of a combination of surname before marriage and husband's surname. Enter under the first element of the compound surname unless the person's language is Portuguese. If the person's language is Portuguese, enter under the last element.

[22.5C4]

> **Johnson Smith, Geoffrey**

> **Hungry Wolf, Adolf**

> **Cotarelo y Mori, Emilio**

but **Silva, Ovidio Saraiva de Carvalho e**

3.5C5. Other compound surnames. Married women whose surname consists of surname before marriage and husband's surname. Enter under the first element of the compound surname (regardless of its nature) if the woman's language is Czech, French, Hungarian, Italian, or Spanish. In all other cases, enter under the husband's surname. For hyphenated names, see 3.5C3.

[22.5C5]

> **Bonacci Brunamonti, Alinda**
> (*Language of person: Italian*)

> **Molina y Vedia de Bastianini, Delfina**
> (*Language of person: Spanish*)

> **Stowe, Harriet Beecher**
> (*Language of person: English*)

> **Wang Ma, Hsi-ch'un**
> (*Language of person: Chinese*)

---

6. Disregard reference sources that list compound surnames in a uniform style regardless of preference or customary usage.

3.5C6 HEADINGS FOR PERSONS

3.5C6. Nature of surname uncertain. If a name has the appearance of a compound surname but its nature is not certain, treat it as a compound surname unless the language of the person is English or one of the Scandinavian languages.

If the person's language is English, enter under the last part of the name and do not refer from the preceding part unless the name as been treated as compound surname in reference sources.

[22.5C6]

> **Adams, John Crawford**
>
> **Lee, Joseph Jenkins**

3.5C7. Words indicating relationship following surnames. Treat the words *Filho, Junior, Neto, Netto,* or *Sobrinho* following a Portuguese surname as part of the surname. Omit similar terms (Jr., Sr., etc.) occurring in all other languages unless required to distinguish between two or more identical names (see 3.16B).

[22.5C8]

3.5D. Surnames with separately written prefixes

3.5D1. Articles and prepositions. If a surname includes an article or preposition or combination of the two, enter under the element most commonly used as entry element in alphabetically arranged directories, etc., in the person's language or country of residence or activity. For specific guidelines and examples in various languages and language groups other than English and French, see AACR 2 rule 22.5D1.

[22.5D1]

ENGLISH. Enter under the prefix.

> **De Morgan, Augustus**
>
> **De la Mare, Walter**
>
> **Du Maurier, Daphne**
>
> **Le Gallienne, Richard**
>
> **Van Buren, Martin**
>
> **Von Braun, Wernher**

FRENCH. If the prefix consists of an article or of a contraction of an article and a preposition, enter under the prefix.

> **Le Rouge, Gustave**
>
> **La Bruyère, René**
>
> **Du Méril, Édélestand Pontas**
>
> **Des Granges, Charles-Marc**

3.5D2. Other prefixes. If the prefix is not an article, or preposition, or combination of the two, enter under the prefix.

[22.5D2]

> **À Beckett, Gilbert Abbott**

Ap Rhys Price, Henry Edward

Ben Maÿr, Berl

3.5E. Prefixes hyphenated or combined with surnames

3.5E1. If the prefix is regularly or occasionally hyphenated or combined with the surname, enter the name under the prefix. As required, refer from the part of the name following the prefix.

[22.5E1]

FitzGerald, David

MacDonald, William

Debure, Guillaume
   x Bure, Guillaume de

Fon-Lampe, A. A.
   x Lampe, A. A. Fon-

3.5F. Members of royal houses entered under surname, etc.

3.5F1. Enter the name of a member of a royal house no longer reigning or of a royal house that has lost or renounced its throne, and who is no longer identified as royalty, under surname or the part of the name by which he or she is identified in his or her works, or in reference sources (e.g., name of the house or dynasty, territorial title) if there is no surname. Add titles that the person still uses as instructed in 3.10. Refer from the given name followed by the title as instructed in 3.13A1-3.13A4.

[22.5F1]

Habsburg, Otto
   x Otto, *Archduke of Austria*

Hohenzollern, Franz Joseph, *Fürst von*
   x Franz Joseph, *Prince of Hohenzollern*

Paris, Henri, *comte de*
   x Henri, *Count of Paris*

Wied, Maximilian, *Prinz von*
   x Maximilian, *Prince of Wied*

3.6. ENTRY UNDER TITLE OF NOBILITY

3.6A. General rule

3.6A1. Enter under the proper name in a title of nobility (including courtesy titles) if the person is commonly known by that title. Apply this rule to persons who:

    (a) use their titles rather than their surnames in their works

 or   (b) are listed under their titles in reference sources.

Follow the proper name in the title by the personal name (excluding unused forenames) in direct order and the term of rank[7] in the vernacular. Omit the surname and term of rank if the person does not use a term of rank or a substitute for it. Refer from the surname unless the proper name in the title is the same as the surname.[8]

[22.6A1]

Byron, George Gordon Byron, *Baron*

Macaulay, Thomas Babington Macaulay, *Baron*

Nairne, Carolina Nairne, *Baroness*

Bolingbroke, Henry St. John, *Viscount*

Cavour, Camillo Benso, *conte di*

Willoughby de Broke, Richard Greville Verney, *Baron*

3.6B. Special rules

3.6B1. Some titles in the United Kingdom peerage include a territorial designation that may or may not be an integral part of the title. If the territorial designation is an integral part of the title, include it.

[22.6B1]

Russell of Liverpool, Edward Frederick Langley Russell, *Baron*

If it is not an integral part of the title, or if there is doubt that it is, omit it.

	Bracken, Brendan Bracken, *Viscount*
not	Bracken of Christchurch, Brendan Bracken, *Viscount*

3.6B2. Apply 3.6A1 to judges of the Scottish Court of Session bearing a law title beginning with *Lord*.

[22.6B2]

Kames, Henry Home, *Lord*
    x Home, Henry, *Lord Kames*

3.6B3. If a person acquires a title of nobility, disclaims such a title, or acquires a new title of nobility, follow the instructions in 3.2C in choosing the name to be used as the basis for the heading.

[22.6B3]

---

7. The terms of rank in the United Kingdom peerage are duke, duchess, marquess (marquis), marchioness, earl, countess, viscount, viscountess, baron, and baroness. The heir of a British peer above the rank of baron usually takes the next to highest title of the peer during the peer's lifetime.

8. Note that the application of the basic provisions of this rule often results in a form of name for a person of nobility that is not the form most commonly found in the chief sources of information of that person's published works. The first and second sentence of the rule apply the basic provisions of 3.1A-3.1B to nobility. Therefore, the Duke of Wellington whose personal name was Arthur Wellesley, is entered under the proper name of the title, i.e., *Wellington*. The third sentence gives instructions for formulating the name: follow the proper name in the title by the person's personal name in direct order and follow the personal name by the term of rank. Application of this rule to the Duke of Wellington results in the heading *Wellington, Arthur Wellesley, Duke of* despite the fact that *Duke of Wellington* is the form of name by which he is commonly known under the provisions of 3.1A-3.1B.

Caradon, Hugh Foot, *Baron*
(*Previously* Sir Hugh Foot)

George-Brown, George Brown, *Baron*
(*Previously* George Brown)

Hailsham of St. Marylebone, Quintin Hogg, *Baron*
(*Originally* Quintin Hogg; *became* Viscount Hailsham, *1950;
peerage disclaimed, 1963; became* Baron Hailsham of St.
Marylebone, *1970*)

3.7. ENTRY UNDER GIVEN NAME, ETC.

3.7A. General rule

3.7A1. Enter a name that does not include a surname and that is borne by a person who is
not identified by a title of nobility under the part of the name under which the person is
listed in reference sources. Include in the name any words or phrases denoting place of
origin, domicile, occupation, or other characteristic that are commonly associated with
the name in works by the person or in reference sources. Precede such words or phrases
by a comma, unless the name cannot easily be broken down into "name" and "phrase"
components.

[22.8A1; RI]

John, *the Baptist*

Leonardo, *da Vinci*

John of the Cross

3.7A2. If a person with such a name is listed in reference sources by a part of the name
other than the first, follow the instructions in 3.5B.

[22.8A2]

Planudes, Maximus

Helena, Maria

3.7B. Names of royal persons

3.7B1. If the name by which a royal person is known includes the name of a royal house,
dynasty, territorial designation, etc., or a surname, enter the name in direct order. Add
titles as instructed in 3.13A.

[22.8C1]

John II Comnenus...

Louis Bonaparte...

Daulat Rao Sindhia...

Ming T'ai-tsu...

Eleanor, *of Aquitaine*...

3.8. ENTRY UNDER INITIALS, LETTERS, OR NUMERALS

3.8A. Enter a name consisting of initials, or separate letters, or numerals, or consisting primarily of initials, under those initials, letters, or numerals in direct order. Include any typographic devices that follow the letters. Include any words or phrases associated with the initials, letters, or numerals. See also 3.15A.

[22.10A]

H. D.

A. de O.

B..., *abbé de*

D. S., *Master*

3.9. ENTRY UNDER PHRASE

3.9A. Enter in direct order a name that consists of a phrase or other appellation that does not contain a forename.

[22.11A]

Dr. X

Father Time

Pan Painter

Mr. Fixit

Also enter in direct order a phrase that consists of a forename or forenames preceded by words other than a term of address or a title of position or office. Make a reference from the forename(s) followed by the initial word(s).

Buffalo Bill

Typhoid Mary

Poor Richard

If, however, such a name has the appearance of a forename, forenames, or initials, and a surname, enter under the pseudosurname.

Other, A. N.

If such a name does not convey the idea of a person, add in parentheses a suitable general designation in English.

River (*Writer*)

Taj Mahal (*Musician*)

3.9B. If the phrase consists of a forename preceded by a term of address (e.g., a word indicating relationship) or a title of position or office (e.g., a professional appellation), enter under the forename. Treat the other word(s) as additions to the forename(s).

[22.11B]

Fannie, *Cousin*

Jemima, *Aunt*

Pierre, *Chef*

Additions to Names

3.10. TITLE OF NOBILITY AND TERMS OF HONOR

3.10A. Add, to the name of a nobleman or noblewoman not entered under title (see 3.6), the title of nobility in the vernacular if the title or part of the title or a substitute for the title (such as *Lord* or *Lady*) commonly appears with the name in published works by the person or in reference sources.[9] In case of doubt, add the title.

[22.12A]

Bismarck, Otto, *Fürst von*

3.10B. British terms of honor

Add a British term of honor (*Sir*, *Dame*, *Lord*, and *Lady*) if the term commonly appears with the name in published works by the person or in reference sources. In case of doubt, add the term of honor. Add the term at the end of the name.

[22.12B1; RI]

West, Rebecca, *Dame*
(*Person identified by pseudonym*)

Beecham, Thomas, *Sir*
(*Baronet*)

Gordon, George, *Lord*
(*Younger son of a duke*)

but

Christie, Agatha
(*Term of honor* Dame *not used in her works*)

Fraser, Antonia
(*Term of honor* Lady *not used in her works*)

3.11. SAINTS

3.11A. Add *Saint* after the name of a Christian saint, unless the person was a pope, emperor, empress, king, or queen, in which case follow 3.13A-3.13B.

[22.13A]

Alban, *Saint*

Teresa, *of Avila, Saint*

Francis, *of Assisi, Saint*

More, Thomas, *Sir, Saint*

Seton, Elizabeth Ann, *Saint*

3.11B. Add any other suitable word or phrase necessary to distinguish between two saints.

[22.13B]

Augustine, *Saint, Archbishop of Canterbury*

Augustine, *Saint, Bishop of Hippo*

---

9. Disregard, in this context, reference sources dealing with the nobility.

3.12. ADDITIONS TO NAMES ENTERED UNDER SURNAME

3.12A. If the name by which a person is known consists only of a surname, add the word or phrase associated with the name in works by the person or in reference sources. If the person uses only his or her surname, or only a term of address, etc., and a surname, establish the surname without forename(s) as the heading. (However, see 3.6 for persons of nobility who do not use a forename and are entered under the title of nobility.)

[22.15A; RI]

> **Deidier,** *abbé*
>
> **Moses,** *Grandma*
>
> **Read,** *Miss*
>
> **D'Ambrosio**
> (*Name used:* D'Ambrosio; *forenames,* Joseph J. *are known*)

If no such word or phrase exists, make additions to surnames alone only when they are needed to distinguish two or more persons with the same name.

3.12B. Terms of address of married women

Add the term of address of a married woman if she is identified only by her husband's name. To achieve proper filing order in automated systems, add the term of address *after* the name.

[22.15B1; RI]

> **Ward, Humphry,** *Mrs.*

3.13. ADDITIONS TO NAMES ENTERED UNDER GIVEN NAME, ETC.

3.13A. Royalty

3.13A1. Add, to the name of the person with the highest royal status within a state or people, a phrase consisting of a person's title (in English if there is a satisfactory English equivalent) and the name of the state or people in in English.

[22.16A1; RI]

> **Clovis,** *King of the Franks*
>
> **Hirohito,** *Emperor of Japan*
>
> **John,** *King of England*
>
> **Jean,** *Grand Duke of Luxembourg*
>
> **Alfonso XIII,** *King of Spain*
>
> **Elizabeth II,** *Queen of Great Britain*
>
> **Victor Emmanuel II,** *King of Italy*
>
> **Gustaf I Vasa,** *King of Sweden*
>
> **Gustaf II Adolf,** *King of Sweden*

3.13A2. Do not add other epithets associated with the name of such a person. Refer from the name with the epithet(s).

[22.16A2]

> **Louis IX,** *King of France*
>   *x* Louis, *Saint, King of France*
>
> **Constantine I,** *Emperor of Rome*
>   *x* Constantine, *Saint*
>
> **Charles,** *Duke of Burgundy*
>   *x* Charles, *the Bold*
>
> **Catherine II,** *Empress of Russia*
>   *x* Catherine, *the Great*
>
> **Suleiman I,** *Sultan of the Turks*
>   *x* Suleiman, *the Magnificent*

3.13A3. Consorts of royal persons. Add, to the name of a consort of a person with the highest royal status within a state or people, his or her title (in English, if there is a satisfactory English equivalent) followed by *consort of* [the name of the royal person as prescribed in 3.13A1].

[22.16A3]

> **Philip,** *Prince, consort of Elizabeth II, Queen of Great Britain*
>
> **Albert,** *Prince Consort of Victoria, Queen of Great Britain*
>   (*His title was* Prince Consort)
>
> **Ingrid,** *Queen, consort of Frederick IX, King of Denmark*

Epithets commonly associated with the names of consorts of monarchs should be retained in the heading, according to the provisions of 3.7A. (The epithets should not be deleted on analogy with the deletion of such for the monarchs, according to 3.13A2).

[RI]

> **Eleanor,** *of Aquitaine, Queen, consort of Henry II, King of England*
> *not*   Eleanor, *Queen, consort of Henry II, King of England*

3.13A4. Children and grandchildren of royal persons. Add, to the name of a child or grandchild of a person with the highest royal status within a state or people, the title (in English if there is a satisfactory English equivalent) borne by him or her.

[22.16A4]

> **Carlos,** *Prince of Asturias*
>
> **Eulalia,** *Infanta of Spain*

If such a child or grandchild is known only as *Prince* or *Princess* (or a similar title in English or another language) without a territorial designation, add that title (in English if there is a satisfactory English equivalent) followed by:

> a) another title associated with the name
> *or* b) *daughter of..., son of..., granddaughter of...,* or *grandson of...* [the name and title of the parent or grandparent as prescribed in 3.13A1].

> **Margaret,** *Princess, Countess of Snowdon*
>
> **Anne,** *Princess Royal, daughter of Elizabeth II, Queen of Great Britain*

3.13B. Popes
Add *Pope* to a name identifying a pope.

[22.16B1]

        Pius XII, *Pope*

        Gregory I, *Pope*

Add *Antipope* to a name identifying an antipope.

        Clement VII, *Antipope*

3.13C. Bishops, etc.
If a bishop, cardinal, archbishop, metropolitan, abbot, abbess, or other high ecclesiastical official is identified by a given name, add the title (in English if there is a satisfactory English equivalent). If the person has borne more than one such title, give the one of highest rank.

Use *Archbishop* for all archbishops other than cardinals. Use *Bishop* for all bishops other than cardinals. Use *Chorepiscopus* for persons so designated. Use *Cardinal* for cardinal-bishops, cardinal-priests, and cardinal-deacons. Add to the title of a diocesan bishop or archbishop or of a patriarch the name of the latest see, in English if there is an English form.

[22.16C1]

        Bēssariōn, *Cardinal*

        Dositheos, *Patriarch of Jerusalem*

        John, *Bishop of Ephesus*

        Platon, *Metropolitan of Moscow*

[However, religious titles are not added when the person is entered under surname,[10] e.g.:
        Cushing, Richard, 1895-
        Gibbons, James, 1834-1921]

3.14. DATES
Add a person's dates (birth, death, etc.), if known, as the last element of a heading. Record the dates in the form given below.

Give dates in terms of the Christian era. Add *B.C.* when appropriate. Give dates from 1582 on in terms of the Gregorian calendar.[11]

[22.17A]

        Smith, John, 1924-
          (*Living person*)

        Smith, John, 1900 Jan. 10-
        Smith, John, 1900 Mar. 2-
          (*Same name, same year of birth*)

---

10. Most archival and manuscript repositories are more likely to encounter modern-day bishops, archbishops, etc., where entry would be made under surname.

11. The Gregorian calendar was adopted in France, Italy, Portugal, and Spain in 1582; by the Catholic states of Germany in 1583; by the United Kingdom in 1752; by Sweden in 1753; by Prussia in 1774; and by the Russian Republic in 1918. See AACR 2 rule 22.17 (footnote 18) for converting dates in the Julian calendar to the Gregorian calendar.

Smith, John, 1837-1896
Mantovani, 1905-1980
Pliny, the Younger, 62-113
Davies, W. H. (William Henry), 1871-1940
Lindbergh, Charles A. (Charles August), 1859-1924
Lindbergh, Charles A. (Charles Augustus), 1902-1974
Torrance, Ell, 1844-1932
Torrance, Ell, 1878-1940
(Both years known)

Smith, John, 1836 or 7-1896
(Year of birth uncertain between consecutive years)

Smith, John, 1837?-1896
(Authorities differ as to year of birth; 1837 probable)

Ovid, 43 B.C.-17 or 18 A.D.
(Authorities differ as to year of death)

Smith, John, ca. 1837-1896
(Year of birth uncertain by several years)

Smith, John, 1837-ca. 1896
(Year of death approximate)

Smith, John, ca. 1837-ca. 1896
(Both years approximate)

Smith, John, *b.* 1825
(Year of death unknown)

Smith, John, *d.* 1859
(Year of birth unknown)

Johnson, Carl F., *fl.* 1893-1896
Joannes, *Diaconus, fl.* 1226-1240
(Years of birth and death unknown. Some years of activity known. Do not use flourish (fl.) dates for the 20th century.)

3.15. FULLER FORMS

3.15A. If part or all of a name is represented by initials and the full form is known, add the spelled out form in parentheses. When adding the full form, observe the following guidelines:

[22.18A; RI]

1) If the initial occurs in the forename portion of the surname-forename heading, give in the parenthetical addition not only the full form but also the other forenames that appear in the forename portion of the heading. Place the parenthetical addition directly after the forename portion and before any other additions (e.g., date, title).

    Flam, F. A. (Floyd A.)

    Smith, T. B. (T. Basil)

Wright, G. H. von (Georg Henrik), 1916-

Smith, Arthur D. (Arthur Dwight), 1907-

Bvindi, Francis A. A. L. (Francis A. A. Lovemore), 1955-

2) If the initial occurs in the surname portion of the surname-forename heading, give in the parenthetical addition not only the full form but also the other surnames that appear in the surname portion of the heading. Place the parenthetical addition directly after the forename portion as in 1) above.

Rodríguez H., Guadalupe (Rodríguez Hernández)

3) If an initial occurs in both the forename and surname portions in a surname-forename heading, give in the parenthetical addition all the names that appear in the heading and in running form. Place the parenthetical addition directly after the forename portion as in 1) above.

González R., Pedro F. (Pedro Felipe González Rodríguez)

4) If the initial occurs in the name entered as a given name, etc., give in the parenthetical addition all the names that appear in the heading. Place the parenthetical addition directly after the given name and before any additions (e.g. date, title).

M. Alicia (Mary Alicia), *Sister, S.C.N.*

5) If the heading consists solely of initials (see 3.8), give in the parenthetical addition the full form if there is no doubt what the initials stand for.

H. D. (Hilda Doolittle), 1886-1961

Do not apply guideline number 5 to a heading for a married woman that consists of her husband's surname and initials.

Renfro, Roy E., *Mrs.*
not   Renfro, Roy E. (Roy Edward), *Mrs.*

6) For names that are represented in the heading by an abbreviation rather than an initial, give in the parenthetical addition the full name for the person.

Brownridge, Wm. (William)

3.16. DISTINGUISHING TERMS

3.16A. Names in which the entry element is a given name, etc.

If neither a fuller form of name nor dates are available to distinguish between identical headings of which the entry element is a given name, etc., devise a suitable brief term and add it in parentheses.

[22.19A]

Johannes (*Notary*)

Thomas (*Anglo-Norman poet*)

Charles (*Blacksmith of Wake County, N.C.*)

3.16B. Names in which the entry element is a surname

If neither a fuller form of name nor dates are available to distinguish between identical headings of which the entry element is a surname, add a qualifier (e.g., term of address, title of position or office, initials of an academic degree, initials denoting membership in an organization) that appears with the name in works by the person or in reference sources.

[22.19B1]

Brown, George, *Captain*

Saur, Karl-Otto, *Jr.*

Baker, *Miss, of Falls Church, Va.*

Falkland, Leonard, *Blacksmith of Elsah, Ill.*

Stevens, Samuel, *Ph. D.*

Interpretation

Terms of address, etc., for pre-20th century persons. For persons who lived primarily before the 20th century, interpret "with the name" loosely, and combine the term, title, etc., with the name so long as both are found, whether together or not, in works or material by the person or in reference sources. Apply this to names entered under given name, initials, etc. (3.16A), and under surname (3.16B).

[RI]

Examples:

In chief source:	a merchant of York
Found within work:	T. H.
Heading:	**T. H.** (*Merchant of York*) *(Name entered under initials; addition in parentheses)*

In chief source:	Will Dyer
Found within work:	wool merchant
Heading:	**Dyer, Will,** *wool merchant* *(Name entered under surname; addition not in parentheses)*

3.17. UNDIFFERENTIATED NAMES

If no suitable addition (fuller form of name, dates, or distinguishing term) is available, use the same heading for all persons with the same name.

[22.20]

CHAPTER 4

GEOGRAPHIC NAMES

Contents

4.1. INTRODUCTORY NOTE

The names of geographic entities (referred to throughout this chapter as "places") are used to distinguish between corporate bodies with the same name (see 5.4C); as additions to other corporate names (e.g. conference names, see 5.7B4); and, commonly, as the names of governments (see 5.3E) and communities that are not governments.

[23.1A]

4.2. GENERAL RULES

4.2A. English form

Use the English form of the name of a place if there is one in general use. Determine this from gazetteers and other reference sources published in English-speaking countries. In case of doubt, use the vernacular form (see 4.2B).

[23.2A1]

	Austria
not	Österreich
	Copenhagen
not	København
	Florence
not	Firenze
	Ghent
not	Gent
not	Gand
	Sweden
not	Sverige

If the English form of the name of a place is the English name of the government that has jurisdiction over the place, use that form.

Soviet Union
not   Soĭuz Sovetskikh Sotsialisticheskikh Republik
not   Russia
not   Union of Soviet Socialist Republics
(*U.S. Board on Geographic Names approves both* Soviet Union *and* Union of Soviet Socialist Republics; *prefer the former*)

[RI]

4.2B. Vernacular form

4.2B1. Use the form in the official language of the country if there is no English form in general use.

[23.2B1]

Buenos Aires

Gorlovka

Tallinn

Livorno
not   Leghorn
(*English form no longer in general use*)

If the country has more than one official language, use the form most commonly found in English-language sources.

[23.2B2]

Louvain
not   Leuven

Helsinki
not   Helsingfors

Interpretations

4.2C. Sources
Apply the following for current place names:

a)   For names in the United States, base the heading on the form found in a recent edition of the *Rand McNally Commercial Atlas and Marketing Guide.*

b)   For names in Great Britain, Australia, and New Zealand, base the heading on the form found in a recently published gazetteer.

c)   For names in Canada, use the heading provided by the National Library of Canada. Accept the NLC form, even if it differs from LC policy in such matters as abbreviations, fullness, qualifiers, etc.

d)   For other names, base the heading either on the form found in the material being cataloged together with a consideration of the form found in a recently published gazetteer, *or*, on the form provided by the U.S. Board on Geographic Names (BGN), as necessary. In cases of conflict between BGN practice with regard to vernacular forms and romanization, prefer English forms to vernacular and Library of Congress romanization practice.

[RI]

4.2D. English or vernacular forms

If BGN approves both a vernacular and an English form (called a conventional name in BGN terminology), use the English form.

Note: If a foreign name is established in an English form, use the same form whenever the name is used by more than one jurisdictional level or is used as part of another name.

[RI]

	Kyoto (*Japan*)
	Kyoto (*Japan : Prefecture*)
not	Kyoto-fu (Japan)
	Cologne (*Germany*)
	Cologne-Deutz (*Cologne, Germany*)
not	Köln-Deutz (Cologne, Germany)

4.2E. Modifications of the name

4.2E1. Initial articles

Drop initial articles from the beginning of the entry element of geographic names in Arabic, Urdu, Hebrew, and Yiddish. Retain initial articles in other non-English geographic names when retention is supported by current gazetteers in the country's language. "Non-English" is meant to include names in French, Spanish, etc., when these are used in the United States (e.g., Los Angeles) or other English-speaking countries. Drop all other initial articles (e.g., drop *The* from *The Dalles*).

[RI]

4.2E2. Forms found in gazetteers

If the name is based on the form found in a recently published gazetteer, generally use in the heading the form found on the item at hand rather than a shortened form or unabbreviated form found in a gazetteer, unless 4.5A is applicable. However, for *Saint* or *St.* and *Mount* or *Mt.*, always use the spelled out form regardless of the item in hand or other evidence.

[RI]

In source:	Montgomery County
Gazetteer:	Montgomery
Heading:	**Montgomery County** (*Md.*)
In source:	St. Joseph
Gazetteer:	Saint Joseph
Heading:	**Saint Joseph** (*Mo.*)

4.2E3. Districts of India

In order to have consistent headings for the districts of India, establish all of them with the word *District* (or its equivalent in non-English) omitted. If the resulting headings conflict, as in the case of the city's bearing the same name, add *District* as an element of the parenthetical qualifier (see 5.6).

[RI]

4.2E4. U.S. townships

For U.S. townships (called "towns" in New England and some other states), do not include *township* (or *town*) as part of the name used in the heading. If the name of such an entity conflicts with the name of another place in the same state, apply 4.4F1 if the conflict is with the name of another township or 5.6C if the other place is not a township.

[RI]

4.2F. Special decisions

CHINA

For all the governments that have controlled the mainland of China use *China* for all periods except 1931-1945. For the period 1931-1945, use one of the following headings, as appropriate.

China
(*For the government headquartered in Nanking, 1931-1937, and in Chungking, 1937-1945*)

China (*Soviet Republic, 1931-1937*)
(*For the government headquartered in Jui-chin, 1931-1937*)

China (*Provisional government, 1937-1940*)
(*For the government headquartered in Peking, 1937-1940*)

China (*Reformed government, 1938-1940*)
(*For the government headquartered in Nanking, 1938-1940*)

China (*National government, 1940-1945*)
(*For the government headquartered in Nanking, 1940-1945*)

For the post-1948 government on Taiwan, use

China (*Republic, 1949-*)

For the province of Taiwan, use

Taiwan

GERMANY

For the Federal Republic of Germany use

Germany (*West*)

For the German Democratic Republic, use

Germany (*East*)

GREAT BRITAIN

For the United Kingdom, use

Great Britain

KOREA

For the Democratic People's Republic of Korea, use

Korea (*North*)

For the Republic of Korea, use

Korea (*South*)

LONDON
   In dealing with London, use the following headings:

   1.   Use **Corporation of London** for items from the entity bearing this name
        that has administrative control over the 677-acre City of London.

   2.   Use **Greater London Council** for items from the former entity bearing
        this name that had administrative control over the 32 London boroughs
        which made up "Greater London" (excluding the City of London). (The
        entity ceased 1 April 1986).

   3.   Use **London** (*England*) as the qualifier added to corporate headings
        (even though the body concerned is located in a borough or in the City of
        London) or as the entry element for cross references from place.

SOVIET UNION
   For the constituent republics of the Soviet Union, use the following headings:

Armenian S.S.R.	**Lithuania**
Azerbaijan S.S.R.	**Moldavian S.S.R.**
Byelorussian S.S.R.	**Russian S.F.S.R.**
Estonia	**Tajik S.S.R.**
Georgian S.S.R.	**Turkmen S.S.R.**
Kazakh S.S.R.	**Ukraine**
Kirghiz S.S.R.	**Uzbek S.S.R.**
Latvia	

WASHINGTON, D.C.
   Use

District of Columbia

as the heading for the government of this name.
   Use

Washington (D.C.)

only as a location qualifier or as the entry element of cross references from
place.

                                                                              [RI]

4.2G. Military installations

   Treat a military installation as a local place. This means adding as a qualifier the
country, state, province, etc., that would have been added to a city or town in the same
place. Apply this even if the installation is located outside the country that controls it, i.e.,
add the heading for the larger place in which it is located in all cases. Make references
from the name as a subheading of the military branch to which it belongs. (Military installations that are treated as local places include forts, bases, camps, airfields, arsenals,
and Coast Guard stations but not shipyards.)

                                                                              [RI]

March Air Force Base (*Calif.*)
   x March Field (Calif.)
   x United States. March Air Force Base
   x United States. Air Force. March Air Force Base

Yokosuka Naval Base (*Japan*)
    x United States. Yokosuka Naval Base
    x United States. Navy. Yokosuka Naval Base

4.2H. Airports

Establish the heading for an airport according to the provisions for establishing a city or town. Disregard the fact that the airport may be located within a city or town, i.e., do not treat the airport as a place within a city. If the airport and the city with which it is associated are in different larger jurisdictions, add the jurisdiction in which the airport is located.

[RI]

San Francisco International Airport (*Calif.*)

Logan International Airport (*Mass.*)

Jan Smuts Airport (*South Africa*)

Greater Cincinnati International Airport (*Ky.*)

4.3. CHANGES OF NAME

If the name of a place changes, use as many of the names as are required by:

[23.3A]

    a) the rules on government names (5.3E) (e.g., use *Nyasaland* or *Malawi*, as appropriate)
or b) the rules on additions to corporate names (5.4C6) and conference names (5.7B4) (e.g., use *Léopoldville* or *Kinshasa* as appropriate)
or c) other relevant rules in chapter 5.

4.4. ADDITIONS

4.4A. Punctuation

4.4A1. Make all additions to place names used as entry elements (see 5.3E) in parentheses.

[23.4A1]

Budapest (*Hungary*)[1]

If the place name is being used as an addition, precede the name of a larger place by a comma.

Magyar Nemzeti Galéria (*Budapest, Hungary*)[1]

4.4B. General rule

4.4B1. Add to the name of a place (other than a country or a state, etc., listed in 4.4C1 or 4.4D1) the name of a larger place as instructed in 4.4C-4.4F. For additional instructions on distinguishing between place names used as the headings for governments, see 5.6. For instructions on abbreviating some place names used as additions, see AACR 2, Appendix B.14.

[23.4B1]

---

1. This example is included solely to show punctuation patterns. For the construction of the headings, see rules later in this chapter and chapter 5.

Interpretations

ISLANDS AND ISLAND GROUPS

Add to the name of an island or island group that is a jurisdiction the name of the larger jurisdiction only when the island or island group is located near the larger jurisdiction and is commonly associated with it. Otherwise, do not add the name of the larger jurisdiction. In case of doubt, do not add the larger jurisdiction.

[RI]

	Crete (*Greece*)
	Sicily (*Italy*)
	Svalbard (*Norway*)
but	**Greenland**
not	Greenland (Denmark)
	Madeira Islands
not	Madeira Islands (Portugal)
	Réunion
not	Réunion (France)

For places on islands, see 4.4F2.

CHOICE OF LARGER PLACE

When adding the name of a larger place as a qualifier, use the heading for the current name of the larger place. If the smaller place existed when the larger place had an earlier name, and the name in the item pertains to the earlier period, make a reference from the form that shows the earlier name of the larger place if the qualifier is appropriate for the smaller place.

[RI]

Kinshasa (*Zaire*)
    x Kinshasa (Congo)

Charles Town (*W. Va.*)
    x Charles Town (Va.)

If the smaller place has changed its name or has ceased to exist, use as a qualifier the name the larger place had during the period in which the name of the smaller place is applicable.

	Tananarive (*Malagasy Republic*)
not	Tananarive (Madagascar)

FORM OF LARGER PLACE

If the heading for the larger place being added to the smaller place is established according to the provisions of 5.6, do not include in the qualifier the additions prescribed in 5.6.

[RI]

	Albany (*N.Y.*)
not	Albany (N.Y. (State))

76

> **Seoul** (*Korea*)
> *not*   Seoul (Korea (South))

Exception: For Berlin as a government use

> **Berlin** (*Germany*)

before 1949. After 1948 use

> **Berlin** (*Germany : East*)
> *or*   **Berlin** (*Germany : West*)

as appropriate. However, use

> **Berlin** (*Germany*)

as the qualifier in all cases when Berlin is being added to a corporate name heading (5.4C), unless the corporate names conflict.

4.4C. Places in Australia, Canada, Malaysia, United States, U.S.S.R., or Yugoslavia

4.4C1. States, etc. Do not make any addition to the name of a state, province, territory, etc., of Australia, Canada, Malaysia, the United States, the U.S.S.R., or Yugoslavia.

[23.4C1]

> **Northern Territory**
>
> **Prince Edward Island**
>
> **District of Columbia**

4.4C2. Other places. If the place is in a state, province, territory, etc., of one of the countries listed above, add the name of the state, etc., in which it is located.

[23.4C2]

> **Darwin** (*N.T.*)
>
> **Jasper** (*Alta.)*
>
> **George Town** (*Pinang)*
>
> **Cook County** (*Ill.)*
>
> **Alexandria** (*Va.)*
>
> **Washington** (*D.C.)*
>
> **Kiev** (*Ukraine*)
>
> **Split** (*Croatia*)

4.4D. Places in the British Isles

4.4D1. Do not make any additions to the names of the following parts of the British Isles: England, the Republic of Ireland, Northern Ireland, Scotland, Wales, the Isle of Man, the Channel Islands.

[23.4D1]

4.4D2. If a place is located in England, the Republic of Ireland, Northern Ireland, Scotland, Wales, the Isle of Man, or the Channel Islands, add *England*, *Ireland*, *Northern Ireland*, *Scotland*, *Wales*, *Isle of Man*, or *Channel Islands*, as appropriate.

[23.4D2]

> **Dorset** (*England*)
>
> **Pinner** (*England*)
>
> **Clare** (*Ireland*)
>
> **Waterville** (*Ireland*)
>
> **Bangor** (*Northern Ireland*)
>
> **Strathclyde** (*Scotland*)
>
> **Melrose** (*Scotland*)
>
> **Powys** (*Wales*)
>
> **Bangor** (*Wales*)
>
> **Ramsey** (*Isle of Man*)
>
> **Jersey** (*Channel Islands*)

4.4E. Other places

4.4E1. Add to the names of places not covered by 4.4C-4.4D the name of the country in which the place is located.

[23.4E1]

> **Formosa** (*Argentina*)
>
> **Luanda** (*Angola*)
>
> **Lucca** (*Italy*)
>
> **Madras** (*India*)
>
> **Monrovia** (*Liberia*)
>
> **Næsby** (*Denmark*)
>
> **Paris** (*France*)
>
> **Toledo** (*Spain*)

ISRAEL, JORDAN, SYRIA

Do not add the name of the country to places that prior to 1967 were in Jordan or Syria and that are currently within the administered territories of Israel.

[RI]

For Jerusalem, use **Jerusalem**.

SOUTH AFRICA

Add (*South Africa*) to the headings for the South African homelands and to jurisdictions within the homelands. Apply this both to the homelands that South Africa has converted to sovereign nations (e.g., Bophuthatswana) and to those that are currently called self governing territories within South Africa (e.g., Gazankulu).

[RI]

4.4F. Further additions

4.4F1. Distinguishing between otherwise identical place names. If the addition of a larger place as instructed in 4.4C-4.4E is insufficient to distinguish between two or more places with the same name, include a word or phrase commonly used to distinguish them.

[23.4F1]

> **Villaviciosa de Asturias** (*Spain*)
>
> **Villaviciosa de Córdoba** (*Spain*)

If there is no such word or phrase, give an appropriate smaller place before the name of the larger place.

> **Friedberg** (*Bavaria, Germany*)
>
> **Friedberg** (*Hesse, Germany*)
>
> **Tarbert** (*Strathclyde, Scotland*)
>
> **Tarbert** (*Western Isles, Scotland*)
>
> **Basildon** (*Essex, England*)
>
> **Basildon** (*Berkshire, England*)
>
> **Saint Anthony** (*Hennepin County, Minn.*)
>
> **Saint Anthony** (*Stearns County, Minn.*)

Interpretation

Conflicts

Apply either 4.4F1 or 5.6B (depending on the situation) to resolve conflicts in headings for places (geographic names and names of governments) not already resolved by the additions called for by 4.4C-4.4E. Conflict in place names is not restricted to those already established or being established in the catalog (the file against which the searching and cataloging is being done). Instead, if there is no existing conflict in the catalog, search gazetteers, etc., to determine if two or more places within the same jurisdiction have the same name or if two or more places with the same name would bear the same qualifier for the larger place.

U.S. TOWNSHIPS

If a name of a U.S. township (called "towns" in New England and some other states) conflicts with the name of another township within the same state, add the heading for the county to each name.

> **Spring** (*Berks County, Pa.*)
>
> **Spring** (*Centre County, Pa.*)

If the name of a U.S. township conflicts with the name of a place that is not a township, and both are within the same state, apply 5.6C.

HAWAII

If local places in Hawaii conflict, add to each name the heading for the island on which the place is located rather than the heading for the county.

[RI]

4.4F2. Identifying places. If considered necessary to identify the place (as in the case of a community within a city), give the name of an appropriate smaller place before the name of the larger place specified as an addition by the preceding rules.

[23.4F2]

> **Hyde Park** (*Chicago, Ill.*)
>
> **Chelsea** (*London, England*)
>
> **Everton** (*Liverpool, England*)
>
> **Saint Peter Port** (*Guernsey, Channel Islands*)
>
> **Palermo** (*Sicily, Italy*)
>
> **Swansea** (*Toronto, Ont.*)
>
> **11ᵉ Arrondissement** (*Paris, France*)
>
> **Minato-ku** (*Tokyo, Japan*)

Interpretations

PLACES ON ISLANDS

Places on islands in Australia, Canada, Malaysia, United States, U.S.S.R., Yugoslavia, or the British Isles. For places on islands covered by 4.4C or 4.4D, add the qualifier called for by 4.4C2 or 4.4D2.

> **Avalon** (*Calif.*)
>
> **Beaumaris** (*Wales*)

Places on other islands. For places on islands not covered by 4.4C or 4.4D, add the established form for the name of the island or island group if the heading for the island does not contain the name of the country as qualifier. If, however, the heading for the island is qualified by the name of the country, add only the name of the country to the place on the island.

	Naujat (*Greenland*)
not	Naujat (*Denmark*)
	Funchal (*Madeira Islands*)
not	Funchal (*Portugal*)
	Grand Fond (*Réunion*)
not	Grand Fond (*France*)
but	
	Hērakleion (*Greece*)
not	Hērakleion (*Crete, Greece*)

Marsala (*Italy*)

not   Marsala (*Sicily, Italy*)

Longyearbyen (*Norway*)

not   Longyearbyen (*Svalbard, Norway*)

PLACES IN CITIES

For named parts of cities, add the established form for the name of the city. Use the heading reflecting its current status for the entire period of the place's existence (including any earlier independent existence it may have had), provided the name remains constant. Make a reference from the name of the part as a subheading of the name of the city.

Borgfelde (*Hamburg, Germany*)
      x Hamburg (Germany). Borgfelde

If the place once had an independent existence but changed its name when it was absorbed into the larger place, establish a heading for each name.

Endersbach (*Germany*)
      (*For items issued before 1975*)

Weinstadt-Endersbach (*Weinstadt, Germany*)
      (*For items issued after 1974*)
      x Weinstadt (Germany). Weinstadt-Endersbach

If the city part is within another city part, add the name of the city, not the name of the part.

Wahn (*Cologne, Germany*)
      x Cologne (Germany). Wahn

not   Wahn (Porz, Cologne, Germany)

4.5. PLACE NAMES INCLUDING OR REQUIRING A TERM INDICATING A TYPE OF JURISDICTION

4.5A. If the first part of a place name is a term indicating a type of jurisdiction and the place is commonly listed under another element of its name in lists published in the language of the country in which it is located, omit the term indicating the type of jurisdiction.

[23.5A]

Kerry (*Ireland*)

not   County Kerry (*Ireland*)

Ostholstein (*Germany*)

not   Kreis Ostholstein (*Germany*)

In all other cases include the term indicating the type of jurisdiction.

Mexico City (*Mexico*)

Città di Castello (*Italy*)

Ciudad Juárez (*Mexico*)

> **District of Columbia**
>
> **Distrito Federal** (*Brazil*)

4.5B. If a place name does not include a term indicating a type of jurisdiction and such a term is required to distinguish that place from another of the same name, follow the instructions in 5.6.

[23.5B]

CHAPTER 5

HEADINGS FOR CORPORATE BODIES

Contents

Additions, Omissions, and Modifications

Subordinate and Related Bodies

Special Rules

Government Bodies and Officials

Special Rules

Religious Bodies and Officials

5.1. BASIC RULE

Enter a corporate body[1] directly under the name by which it is commonly identified, except when the rules that follow provide for entering it under the name of a higher or related body (see 5.13) or under the name of a government (see 5.18).

Determine the form of name by which a corporate body is commonly identified from publications issued by that body in its language (see also 5.3A), or, when this condition does not apply, from reference sources.[2]

If the name of a corporate body consists of or contains initials, regularize the spacing and put one space after an initial that is followed by a word or other element that is not an initial and no space after an initial that is followed by another initial consisting of one letter.

[24.1A]

[In archival practice, the name by which a corporate body is commonly identified is determined (unless already established) by the form (or forms) found in the following sources, in order of preference:

---

1. For definition, see 2.1B1.

2. When the phrase *reference sources* is used in this chapter, it includes books and articles written about a corporate body.

a) the name that appears most frequently in items issued by the body (if any)
b) the name that appears most frequently in the archival materials being described
c) the name that appears most frequently in reference sources.

The form(s) found may be modified by the rules that follow.]

Aslib

Breitkopf & Härtel

British Museum

Carnegie Library of Pittsburgh

Challenger Expedition...[3]

Chartered Insurance Institute

G. Mendel Memorial Symposium...[3]

Light Fantastic Players

MEDCOM

Museum of American Folk Art

Radio Society of Great Britain

Royal Aeronautical Society

Symposium on Cognition...[3]

University of Oxford

Yale University

5.1A. Romanization

If the name of the body is in a language written in a nonroman script, romanize the name according to the table for that language adopted by the cataloging agency.

[24.1B1]

5.1B. Changes of name

If the name of a corporate body has changed (including changes from one language to another), establish a new heading under the new name for material appearing under that name. See also 2.1B3 for guidelines for choosing headings when corporate body name changes have occurred. Refer from the old heading to the new and from the new heading to the old.

[24.1C1]

American Material Handling Society

changed its name to

International Material Management Society

(Make a see also reference under each name)

---

3. For additions to the names of conferences, congresses, expeditions, etc., see 5.7B.

[When a corporate body changes its name a new heading is established for that name. Old and new heading(s) are all valid depending on their application. In archival records that reflect a series of name changes, the practice is to make headings in a given record for all the various names reflected in the described material. The latest name would be used as the basis of the heading for the main entry and all earlier names would be used as the basis of the headings for added entries. All of the names *must* be established according to the other rules in this chapter.]

5.2. VARIANT NAMES. GENERAL RULES

5.2A. Apply this rule if a body uses variant names in items issued by it. Apply the special rules (5.3) as well when they are appropriate.

[24.2A]

5.2B. If variant forms[4] of the name are found in items issued by the body, use the name as it appears in the chief sources of information as opposed to forms found elsewhere in the items.

[24.2B]

If the name of a corporate body appearing in the chief source would require the addition of a 5.4B qualifier, and a variant form appearing elsewhere in the same item would not require such a qualifier, nevertheless use in the heading the form found in the chief source.

[RI]

Heading:	**Aurora** (*Firm*)
Chief source:	Aurora
Variant form:	Aurora, Inc.

5.2C. If variant spellings of the name appear in items issued by the body, use the form resulting from an official change in orthography, or, if this does not apply, use the predominant spelling.

[24.2C]

5.2D. If variant names appear in the chief source of information, use the name that is presented formally. If no form is presented formally, or if all forms are presented formally, use the predominant form of name.

If there is no predominant form, use a brief form (including an initialism or an acronym) that would differentiate between the body and others with the same or similar brief names.

[24.2D]

> **AFL-CIO**
> *not* American Federation of Labor and Congress of Industrial Organizations
>
> **American Philosophical Society**
> *not* American Philosophical Society Held at Philadelphia for Promoting Useful Knowledge

---

4. Variant forms do not include preceding or succeeding names for that body. For these see 5.1B.

Euratom

not   European Atomic Energy Community

Maryknoll Sisters

not   Congregation of the Maryknoll Sisters

Unesco

not   United Nations Educational, Scientific, and Cultural Organization

If, in a body's publications or records, its full form of name and its initials appear together formally, choose the full form for use in the heading. Change the heading if later evidence shows a clear pattern of predominant usage that differs from the heading chosen.

When a corporate name must be established for materials not of or issued by the corporate body, treat the material being cataloged as a reference source. If the material provides both the body's full form of name and its initials, choose the full form for use in the heading, even if the initials appear prominently and the full form does not.

[RI]

If variant forms do not include a brief form that would differentiate two bodies with the same or similar brief names, use the form found in reference sources or the official form, in that order of preference.

[24.2D]

Metropolitan Applied Research Center
(*Official name. Brief form sometimes used by the center,* MARC
Corporation, *is the same as the name of another body located in
New York*)

5.3. VARIANT NAMES. SPECIAL RULES

5.3A. Language
If the name of a corporate body appears in different languages, use the form in the official language of the body.

[24.3A1]

Société historique franco-américaine

not   Franco-American Historical Society

If the body has two or more official languages, one of which is English, use the English form.

[RI]

Canadian Committee on Cataloguing

not   Comité canadien de catalogage

If the body has two or more official languages, none of which is English, use the form in the language predominantly used in publications issued by the body.

[RI]

Schweizerische Landesbibliothek

not   Biblioteca nazionale svizzera
not   Bibliothèque nationale suisse
         (*German is the language used predominantly by the body in its
         publications*)

If the official language of the body is not known, use the form in the official language of the country in which the body is located if the country has a single official language.

If the categories above are not applicable, use the English, French, German, Spanish, or Russian form, in this order of preference. If none of these apply use the form in the language that comes first in English alphabetic order.

[RI]

5.3B. Language. International bodies

If the name of an international body appears in English on publications issued by it, use the English form. In other cases, follow 5.3A.

[24.3B1]

League of Arab States
not   Union des états arabes
not   Jāmiʻat al-Duwal al-ʻArabīyah

European Economic Community
not   Communauté économique européenne
not   Europese Economische Gemeenschap
       [*etc.*]

International Federation of Library Associations and Institutions
not   Fédération internationale des associations de bibliothécaires et des bibliothèques
not   Internationaler Verband der Bibliothekarischen Vereine und Insitutionen
       [*etc.*]

Nordic Association for American Studies
not   Nordisk selskap for Amerikastudier
not   Nordiska sällskapet för Amerikastudier
       [*etc.*]

5.3C. Conventional name

5.3C1. General rule. If a body is frequently identified by a conventional form of name in reference sources in its own language, use this conventional name.

[24.3C1]

Westminster Abbey
not   Collegiate Church of St. Peter in Westminster

Kunstakademiet (*Denmark*)
not   Det Kongelige Danske kunstakademi

5.3C2. Ancient and international bodies.[5] If the name of a body of ancient origin or of one that is international in character has become firmly established in an English form in English language usage, use this English form.

[24.3C2]

---

5. Apply this rule, for example, to religious bodies, fraternal and knightly orders, church councils, and diplomatic conferences. If it is necessary to establish a heading for a diplomatic conference that has no formal name and has not yet acquired a conventional name, use the name found most commonly in periodical articles and newspaper accounts in English. If another name becomes established later, change the heading to that name.

Benedictines

Coptic Church

Franciscans

Knights of Malta

Paris Peace Conference...

Poor Clares

Royal Arch Masons

5.3D. Religious orders and societies

Use the best-known form of name, in English if possible, for a religious order or society. In case of doubt, follow this order of preference:

a) the conventional name by which its members are known in English
b) the English form of name used by units of the order or society located in English-speaking countries
c) the name of the order or society in the language of the country of its origin.

[24.3D]

	Franciscans
not	Ordo Fratum Minorum
not	Order of St. Francis

	Jesuits
not	Societas Jesu
not	Compañía de Jesús
not	Society of Jesus

	Poor Clares
not	Order of St. Clare
not	Second Order of St. Francis
not	Franciscans. *Second Order*

Brothers of Our Lady of the Fields

Community of the Resurrection

	Dominican Nuns of the Second Order of Perpetual Adoration
not	Dominicans. *Second Order of Perpetual Adoration*

	International Society for Krishna Consciousness
not	Hare Krishna Society

5.3E. Governments

Use the conventional name of a government,[6] unless the official name is in common use. The conventional name of a government is the geographic name (see chapter 4) of

---

6. The word *government* is used here to mean the totality of corporate bodies (executive, legislative, and judicial) exercising the powers of a jurisdiction. Treat as a government agency a corporate body known as *government*, or its equivalent in other languages, or a term with similar meaning, that is an executive element of a particular jurisdiction.

the area (e.g., country, province, state, county, municipality, etc.) over which the government exercises jurisdiction. See also 5.6

[24.3E]

France
not   République française

Yugoslavia
not   Socijalisticka Federativna Republika Jugoslavija

Massachusetts
not   Commonwealth of Massachusetts

Nottinghamshire (*England*)
not   County of Nottingham

Arlington (*Mass.*)
not   Town of Arlington

If the official name of the government is in common use, use it.

Metropolitan Corporation of Greater Winnipeg (*Man.*)

Greater London Council

When it is known that a name or phrase represents a body exercising all the powers (or group of powers) of the government, apply the first sentence of footnote 6 and establish only the heading for the government.

[RI]

United States
not   The Executive Branch of the United States Government

If this fact cannot be known or confidently assumed, proceed as follows:

a)   establish the name as one of the agencies of the government if the name sounds like an agency of that government
b)   establish only the heading for the government if the name does not sound like an agency name of the government.

5.3F. Conferences, congresses, meetings, etc.

5.3F1. If, among the variant forms of a conference name appearing in the chief source of information, there is a form that includes the name or abbreviation of the name of a body associated with the meeting to which the meeting is not subordinate, use this form.

[24.3F1]

FAO Hybrid Maize Meeting...

If, however, the name is of a body to which the meeting is subordinate (e.g., the annual meeting of an association), see 5.13, type 6.

5.3F2. If a conference has both a specific name of its own and a more general name as one of a series of conferences, use the specific name.

[24.3F2]

Symposium on Protein Metabolism...
not   Nutrition Symposium...

Symposium on Endocrines and Nutrition...
not   Nutrition Symposium...

5.3G. Local churches, etc.

If variant forms of the name of a local church, cathedral, monastery, convent, abbey, temple, mosque, synagogue, etc., appear in the chief source of information for materials of, or items issued by the body, use the predominant form. If there is no predominant form, follow this order of preference:

1) a name beginning with or consisting of the name of the person(s), object(s), place(s), or event(s) to which the local church, etc., is dedicated or after which it is named.

    All Saints Church...

    Chapelle Saint-Louis...

    Church of the Holy Sepulchre...

    Duomo di Santa Maria Matricolare...

    St. Clement's Church...

    St. Paul's Cathedral...

    Temple Emanu-El...

2) a name beginning with a word or phrase descriptive of a type of local church, etc.

    Abtei Reichenau

    Great Synagogue...

    Jüdische Reformgemeinde in Berlin

    Monasterio de Clarisas...

    Parish Church of Limpsfield

    Unitarian Universalist Church...

3) a name beginning with the name of the place in which the local church, etc., is situated.

    Anerly Society of the New Church

    Beechen Grove Baptist Church...

    English River Congregation of the Church of the Brethren

    Kölner Dom

    Tenafly Presbyterian Church

    Westover Church...

    Winchester Cathedral

For additions to the name of a local church, etc., see 5.10.

[24.3G1]

For an ecclesiastical parish that consists of a single church and that functions in a civil capacity or exercises duties of civil administration, establish separate headings under the name of the parish and under the name of the church.

St. George's Parish (*Stafford County, Va.*)
St. George's Church (*Stafford County, Va.*)

St. David's Parish (*Cheraw, S.C.*)
St. David's Church (*Cheraw, S.C.*)

For an ecclesiastical parish that does not function in a civil capacity and that consists of a single church, do not establish a heading for the parish. Instead, use the heading for the church. In this case, treat the name of the parish as a variant form of the name of the church.

Christ Church (*Fitchburg, Mass.*)
   x Parish of Christ Church (*Fitchburg, Mass.*)

If an ecclesiastical parish consists of two or more churches and/or chapels, apply the following:

a) If the parish exercised duties of civil administration, establish separate headings for the churches and the parish.

b) If the parish did not function in a civil capacity, and if the parish and one of the churches have a name in common, use the heading for the church (as in the example above).

c) If the name of the parish is different from the name of any of the churches, establish a separate heading for the parish. Treat the heading for the parish according to the rules for local churches.

Henrico Parish

Additions, Omissions, and Modifications

5.4. ADDITIONS

5.4A. General rule
Make additions to the name of a corporate body as instructed in 5.4B-5.4C.

For additions to special types of corporate bodies (e.g., governments, conferences), see 5.6-5.11. Enclose in parentheses all additions required by these and other rules in this chapter.

[24.4A1]

5.4B. Names not conveying the idea of a corporate body
If the name alone does not convey the idea of a corporate body, add a general designation in English. In addition, add a more specific qualifier when two or more corporate bodies have the same name and there is no other way to distinguish between them.

[24.4B1; RI]

Apollo 11 (*Spacecraft*)

Bounty (*Ship*)

Franklin (*Aircraft carrier*)
Franklin (*Steamship*)
  (*Two ships of the same name but each of a different type*)

Lexington (*Aircraft carrier : CV6*)
Lexington (*Aircraft carrier : CVA(N) 65*)
  (*Two aircraft carriers with the same name*)

Elks (*Fraternal order*)

Friedrich Witte (*Firm*)

Alabama (*Musical group*)

Bake-Off (*Contest*)

Monty Python (*Comedy troupe*)

Interpretations

Surnames. Generally do not add a general designation qualifier to a corporate name containing two or more surnames (without forenames or without forename initials).

         Morgan and Morgan
not   Morgan and Morgan (*Firm*)

but   **B. Morgan and D. Morgan** (*Firm*)

Performing duets. Do not add a general designation qualifier if the name of a performing duet contains two surnames (with or without forenames or forename initials) or if the name contains two forenames.

         Simon and Garfunkel

         Ian and Sylvia

Initialisms and acronyms. If the name chosen for the heading for a corporate body is composed of letters written in all capital letters (with or without periods between them), add a general designation qualifier to the name (unless 5.4C is applicable).

         CAST (*Group*)

Ships. Add a general designation qualifier to a heading for a ship if the name alone does not convey the idea of a corporate body. If there is any question as to whether there is an appropriate general term, take the term from the item or material being cataloged.

Art galleries. If the name of an art gallery needs a general designation qualifier and 5.4C is not applicable, use the term *Gallery* as a qualifier rather than a more specific term such as *Art gallery*. (Do not use *Gallery* as a qualifier for an art *museum* needing a general designation qualifier.)

         Ellin Mitchell (*Gallery*)

Consultant firms. If the name of a consultant firm consists *solely* of subject words plus the word "consultants" (or its equivalent in other languages), add a general designation qualifier to the name (unless 5.4C is applicable). Do not add such a qualifier if the name contains other elements.

Hospital Maintenance Consultants (*Firm*)

Multiple qualifiers. If the name is eligible for a qualifier under this rule as well as 5.4C (e.g., when the name conflicts), add the general designation qualifier first. Separate the qualifiers by a space, colon, space.

Red Sea (*Restaurant : Washington, D.C.*)

BANAS (*Organization : Indonesia*)

5.4C. Two or more bodies with the same or similar names

5.4C1. General rule. If two or more bodies have the same name, or names so similar that they may be confused, add a word or phrase to each name as instructed in 5.4C2-5.4C9. Add such a word or phrase to any other name if the addition assists in the understanding of the nature or purpose of the body.

Do not include the additions to names of places prescribed in 5.6 when the names of these places are used to indicate the location of corporate bodies.

[24.4C1]

When two or more bodies have the same name, 5.4C requires the addition of a qualifier to each name. Determine that a conflict exists when the AACR 2 name or heading for one body is the same as the AACR 2 name or heading for another body.

[RI]

Arlington Development Center (*Arlington, Tex.*)
(*Independent nongovernment body*)

Arlington Development Center (*Arlington, S.D.*)
Government body belonging to the City of Arlington)

Arlington Development Center (*Infodata, Inc.*)
(*Subordinate nongovernment body*)

Arlington Development Center (*S.D.*)
(*Government body belonging to the State of South Dakota*)

GOVERNMENT BODIES THAT ARE NOT INSTITUTIONS

Definition: According to 5.17, a body whose immediate parent body is the heading for a government, or whose immediate parent body is entered subordinately to the heading for a government, is treated as a government body. A body is treated as a nongovernment body, however, if its immediate parent body is entered under a heading that is not the name of a government.

[RI]

Government body:
National Endowment for the Arts (*U.S.*)
x United States. *National Endowment for the Arts*

Nongovernment body:

Cultural Resources Development Project (*National Endowment for the Arts*)

> *x* National Endowment for the Arts (*U.S.*). *Cultural Resources Development Project*)

When to qualify: If a government body other than an institution (school, library, laboratory, hospital, archive, museum, prison, etc.) is entered under its own name, add the name of the government as a qualifier unless the government's name (or an understandable surrogate of the government's name) is already present in the name. The qualifier is required even if the name includes a proper noun or adjective (other than the name or surrogate cf the name of the name of the government).

Council on International Economic Policy (*U.S.*)

> *x* United States. *Council on International Economic Policy*

Dundee Harbour Trust (*Great Britain*)

> *x* Great Britain. *Dundee Harbour Trust*

but   **Baltimore Redevelopment Corporation**

> *x* Baltimore (Md.). *Redevelopment Corporation*

Form of qualifier: When adding the name of the government as a qualifier, use its catalog-entry form as modified by 5.4A, 5.4C1, second paragraph, and AACR 2 Appendix B.14.

Yu cheng po wu kwan (*China*)

> *x* China (Republic : 1949-   ). *Yu cheng po wu kwan*

not   Yu cheng po wu kwan (China : Republic : 1949-   )

ALL OTHER BODIES

When to qualify: If a nongovernment body or a government institution (school, library, laboratory, archive, museum, prison, etc.) is entered directly under its own name, add a qualifier *if the addition assists in the understanding of the nature or purpose of the body.*

Choice of qualifier: Choose the most *appropriate* qualifier from among the following:

a) the name of the place or jurisdiction that reflects the scope of the body's activities

b) the name of the local place in which the body is located (or the name of the local place that is commonly associated with the body)

c) the name of the higher or related body (for subordinate or related bodies).

Form of qualifier: When adding the name of a place or jurisdiction, use its catalog-entry form as modified by 4.4 (see also 5.4C3).

Rome Historical Society (*Rome, N.Y.*)

not   Rome Historical Society (*Rome (N.Y.)*)

Northside High School (*Saint Joseph, Mich.*)

not   Northside High School (*Saint Joseph, Mich. : Township*)

Protestant Dutch Reformed Church of Flatlands (*New York, N.Y.*)

not   Protestant Dutch Reformed Church of Flatlands (Flatlands, New
          York, N.Y.)

5.4C2. Names of countries, states, provinces, etc. If a body has a character that is national, state, provincial, etc., add the name of the country, state, province, etc., in which it is located.

[24.4C2]

Republican Party (*Ill.*)

Republican Party (*Mo.*)

Democratic Party (*U.S.*)

Governor's Conference on Aging (*N.J.*)

Governor's Conference on Aging (*Ohio*)

Democratic-Farmer-Labor Party (*Minn.*)

Sociedad Nacional de Minería (*Chile*)

Sociedad Nacional de Minería (*Peru*)

If the addition of the name of the country, state, province, etc., does not adequately distinguish bodies of the same name, add a local place name according to the instructions in 5.4C3-5.4C9.

Massachusetts Correctional Institution (*Bridgewater, Mass.*)

Massachusetts Correctional Institution (*Walpole, Mass.*)

5.4C3. Local place names. In the case of any other body, add the name of the local place in which the body is located or that is commonly associated with its name, unless the name of an institution, the date(s) of the body, or other designation (see 5.4C7-5.4C9) provides better identification.

[24.4C3]

When adding the name of a local place to the name of a body, use its catalog-entry form as modified by 4.4A and 5.4C1, second paragraph. Apply this to both directly and indirectly entered bodies.

[RI]

Louisiana Cancer Conference (*2nd : 1958 : New Orleans, La.*)

not   Louisiana Cancer Conference (*2nd : 1958 : New Orleans*)

France. Direction départementale de l'agriculture (*Vaucluse, France*)

not   France. Direction départementale de l'agriculture (*Vaucluse*)

National Buildings Organisation (*India*). **Rural Housing Wing** (*Srinagar, India*)

not   National Buildings Organisation (*India*). Rural Housing Wing (*Srinagar*)

5.4C4. Bodies located outside the British Isles. In the case of a body located outside the British Isles, add the name of the smallest or most specific local political jurisdiction in which the body is located or that is commonly associated with its name (e.g., the name of the city, town, borough).

[24.4C4]

> **Twentieth Century Club** (*Hartford, Conn.*)
>
> **York University** (*Toronto, Ont.*)

If further distinction is necessary, give the name of a particular area within that jurisdiction before the name of the jurisdiction.

> **Saint John's Church** (*Georgetown, Washington, D.C.*)
>
> **Saint John's Church** (*Lafayette Square, Washington, D.C.*)

If the body is not located in, or if it is not associated with the name of, an incorporated municipality, add the geographic name that is most commonly used to specify its location (e.g., the name of an unincorporated community, the name of a city or town in the vicinity, or the name of the county).

> **Washington County Historical Society** (*Washington County, Ark.*)
>
> **Washington County Historical Society** (*Washington County, Md.*)
>
> **Green Lake Lutheran Church** (*Kandiyohi County, Minn.*)
>
> **Lake County Historical Society** (*Lake County, Minn.*)
>
> **Lake County Historical Society** (*Lake County, Ohio*)

If a body located in a specific local jurisdiction is more commonly associated with the name of another city or town or an unincorporated community, prefer the name of that place.

> **École français de papeterie** (*Grenoble, France*)
> (*School is located in St. Martin d'Héres, an incorporated suburb of Grenoble, but is more closely associated with Grenoble*)

5.4C5. Bodies located in the British Isles. In the case of a body located in the British Isles, add either the name of a geographic entity or the name of the smallest or most specific jurisdiction, whichever is more commonly associated with the name of the body.

[24.4C5]

> **Royal Hospital** (*Chelsea, London, England*)
>
> **Saint Barnabas Church of England School** (*Bradwell, England*)
>
> **Bannatyne Club** (*Edinburgh, Scotland*)
>
> **Red Lion Hotel** (*Newport, Wales*)

5.4C6. Change of name of jurisdiction or locality. If the name of the local jurisdiction or geographic locality changes during the lifetime of the body, add the latest name in use in the lifetime of the body.

[24.4C6]

> **Saint Paul Lutheran Church** (*Skokie, Ill.*)
>
> *not*   Saint Paul Lutheran Church (*Niles Center, Ill.*)
>
> (*Church founded in 1881. Place name changed in 1940*)

> **Midlands Museum** (*Zimbabwe*)
>
> *x* Midlands Museum (*Southern Rhodesia*)

> **Fourth Presbyterian Church** (*Bethesda, Md.*)
>
> *x* Fourth Presbyterian Church (*Washington, D.C.*)
>
> (*Founded 1828 in Washington, D.C., moved to Bethesda, Md., in 1957*)

> *but*   **Historisk samfund** (*Christiana, Norway*)
>
> (*Ceased to exist before Christiana became Oslo.*)

5.4C7. Institutions. When adding the name of a higher or related corporate body to a corporate name, give the name of the body in the form and language on which the heading for the body is *based* (not necessarily in the catalog-entry form for the institution). Use in the qualifier the body's current name. However, if a qualifier is added to the name of a body that no longer exists, use in the qualifier the name of the body that was appropriate at the time the body ceased.

[24.4C7; RI]

> **Newman Club** (*Southern State College*)
>
> *not*   Newman Club (*Southern State College (Springfield (S.D.))*

> **Center for Materials Science** (*National Measurement Laboratory*)
>
> *not*   Center for Materials Science (*National Measurement Laboratory (U.S.)*)

If the combination of corporate name plus qualifier actually conflicts with other headings, then give the qualifier in catalog-entry form.

[RI]

> **Newman Club** (*St. Joseph's College (New York, N.Y.)*)

> **Newman Club** (*St. Joseph's College (Philadelphia, Pa.)*)

If the higher or related body is entered subordinately, use either its parent body or its catalog-entry form.

[RI]

> **Institut avtomatiki i èlectrometrii** (*Akademiia Nauk SSSR*)
>
> *x* Akademiia nauk SSSR. Sibirskoe otdelenie. Institut avtomatiki i èlectrometrii

Change an established heading whenever the existing qualifier becomes inappropriate (as when the name used in the qualifier changes or when the name used in the qualifier is no longer associated with the body being qualified).

[RI]

> **Dokumentations-Leitstelle Afrika** (*Institut für Afrika-Kunde*)
>
> *x* Dokumentations-Leitstelle Afrika (*Deutsches Institut für Afrika-Forschung*)
>
> (*The name of the qualifying body changed from Deutsches Institut für Afrika-Forschung to Institut für Afrika-Kunde*)

5.4C8. Year(s). If the name has been used by two or more bodies that cannot be distinguished by place, add the year of founding or the inclusive years of existence.

[24.4C8]

Scientific Society of San Antonio (*1892-1894*)

Scientific Society of San Antonio (*1904-   *)

5.4C9. Other additions. If none of the place name, name of institution, or date(s) is sufficient or appropriate for distinguishing between two or more bodies, add an appropriate general designation in English.

[24.4C9]

Church of God (*Adventist*)

Church of God (*Apostolic*)

5.5. OMISSIONS

5.5A. Initial articles

Omit an initial article unless the intent is to file on the initial article (e.g., a corporate name that begins with an article that is the first part of the name of a person or place).

[24.5A1]

	Club (*London*)
not	The Club (*London*)

	Français de Grande-Bretagne (*Association*)
not	Le Français de Grande-Bretagne (*Association*)

	Library Association
not	The Library Association

but

El Greco Society
Los Angeles County Museum
The Pas Public Library

5.5B. Terms indicating incorporation and certain other terms

5.5B1. Omit an adjectival term indicating incorporation (e.g., *Incorporated, E.V., Ltd.,* etc.) or state ownership of a corporate body, and a word or phrase designating the type of incorporated entity (e.g., *Aktiebolaget, Gesellschaft mit beschränkter Haftung, Kabushiki Kaisha, Societá per azione,* etc.), unless it is an integral part of the name or is needed to make it clear that the name is that of a corporate body. If the adjectival term appears initially or medially in the name, it is *ipso facto* an integral part of the name. (Note that if the term appears initially, it may be inverted when used in the heading if 5.5B2 is also applicable). If the term appears at the end of the name, treat it as a part of the name only if the term is necessary to show that the name refers to a corporate body.

[24.5C1; RI]

American Ethnological Society
(*Without* Inc.)

Automobiltechnische Gesellschaft
(*Without* E.V., *i.e.*, Eingetranger Verein)

Society of Engineers
(*Without* Incorporated)

Compañía Internacional Editora
(*Without* S.a.)

but

Films Incorporated

Peter Davies Limited

Vickers (Aviation) Limited

5.5B2. If such a term is needed to make it clear that the name is that of a corporate body and it occurs at the beginning of the name, transpose it to the end.

[24.5C2]

Elektrometall, Aktiebolaget
not   Aktiebolaget Elektrometall

Hochbauprojektierung Karl-Marx-Stadt, VEB
not   VEB Hochbauprojektierung Karl-Marx-Stadt

5.5B3. Omit abbreviations (e.g., *U.S.S.* and *H.M.S.*) occurring before the name of a ship.

[24.5C4]

Ark Royal (*Ship*)
not   H.M.S. Ark Royal

5.6. Governments. Additions[7]

5.6A. Apply this rule to the names of governments that are not differentiated by the application of 4.4. Make the further additions prescribed here following a space, colon, space, and within the same parentheses that enclose the additions prescribed in 4.4.

[24.6A1]

5.6B. Add the type of jurisdiction in English if other than a city or town. If there is no English equivalent for the vernacular term, use the vernacular term. In case of doubt, use the vernacular term.

[24.6B]

Cork (*Ireland*)

Cork (*Ireland : County*)

Darmstadt (*Germany*)

Darmstadt (*Germany : Landkreis*)

Darmstadt (*Germany : Regierungsbezirk*)

---

7. The examples shown in this rule are included solely illustrate the use of the various additions. The construction of these headings by a particular cataloging agency depends on the application of the options in chapter 4 or on actual need for differentiation in a particular catalog.

Guadalajara (*Mexico*)

Guadalajara (*Spain*)

Guadalajara (*Spain : Province*)

New York (*N.Y.*)

New York (*State*)

Québec (*Québec*)

Québec (*Province*)

Québec (*Québec : County*)

When a sovereign nation and another place of the same name that is not a sovereign nation exist at the same time, do not qualify the name of the sovereign nation.

[RI]

Italy (*Tex.*)

Italy

When a succession of jurisdictions would be entered under the same name, use one heading for all, no matter what differences there are between the jurisdictions.

[RI]

	North Carolina
not	North Carolina (*Colony*)
	North Carolina (*State*)

	Texas
not	Texas (*Republic*)
	Texas (*State*)

	Hawaii
not	Hawaii (*Kingdom*)
	Hawaii (*Republic*)
	Hawaii (*State*)

	India
not	India (*Dominion*)
	India (*Republic*)

However, when the geographical qualifier added to a name to reflect its current status is not appropriate for the earlier entity, use two headings, and qualify each.

[RI]

	Brabant (*Belgium*)
	Brabant (*Duchy*)
not	Brabant (*Belgium*)

	Venice (*Italy*)
	Venice (*Republic*)
not	Venice (*Italy*)

	Tuscany (*Italy*)
	Tuscany (*Grand Duchy*)
not	Tuscany (*Italy*)

          Aragon (*Spain*)
          Aragon (*Kingdom*)
not   Aragon (*Spain*)
but

          Dakota Territory
            x Dakota
            xx South Dakota
            xx North Dakota

When the name of a state, province, or territory in Australia, Canada, or the United States; of a county, region, or islands area in England, Scotland, Wales, or the Republic of Ireland; of a constituent state of Malaysia, the U.S.S.R., or Yugoslavia; or of an island that is a jurisdiction conflicts with the name of a place within the larger jurisdiction, add the type of government as a qualifier to the larger geographic entity.

                                                      [RI]

          New York (*N.Y.*)
          New York (*State*)
not   New York

          Durham (*England*)
          Durham (*England : County*)
not   Durham

When the name of a state, province, or territory in Australia, Canada, or the United States; of a county, region, or islands area in England, Scotland, Wales, or the Republic of Ireland; of a constituent state of Malaysia, the U.S.S.R., or Yugoslavia; or of an island that is a jurisdiction conflicts with the name of a place in another jurisdiction, qualify the latter only.

                                                      [RI]

          Alberta (*Va.*)
          Alberta
not   Alberta (*Province*)

          Victoria (*Tex.*)
          Victoria
not   Victoria (State)

          Virginia (*Minn.*)
          Virginia
not   Virginia (*State*)

Exception: Use

          Washington (*State*)

as the heading for the state of Washington.

5.6C. If the type of jurisdiction does not provide a satisfactory distinction, add an appropriate word or phrase.

                                                    [24.6C]

If the name of a U.S. township (called "towns" in New England and some other states) conflicts, apply the following:

[RI]

1) If the conflict is with the name of a local place within the same state, add

    a) the name of the state to the local place

    b) the name of the state and *Township* (or *Town*) to the name of the township.

        Passaic (*N.J.*)

        Passaic (*N.J. : Township*)

2) If the conflict is with both the name of a local place *and* the name of another township, all of which are within the same state, add

    a) the name of the state to the local place

    b) the name of the county, the name of the state, and *Township* (or *Town*) to the names of the townships.

        Berlin (*Wis.*)

        Berlin (*Green Lake County, Wis. : Town*)

        Berlin (*Marathon County, Wis. : Town*)

3) If the conflict is only with the name of another township within the same state, apply 4.4F.

5.6D. If two or more governments lay claim to jurisdiction over the same area (e.g., as with occupying powers and insurgent governments), add a suitable designation to one or each of the governments, followed by the inclusive years of its existence.

[24.6D]

        France
        France (*Territory under German occupation, 1940-1944*)

        Algeria
        Algeria (*Provisional government, 1958-1962*)

5.7. CONFERENCES, CONGRESSES, MEETINGS, ETC.

5.7A. Omissions

Omit from the name of a conference, etc., indications of its number, frequency, or year(s) of convocation.

[24.7A1]

        Louisiana Cancer Conference...
not   Biennial Louisiana Cancer Conference...

        Conference on Co-ordination of Galactic Research...
not   Second Conference on Co-ordination of Galactic Research...

5.7B. Additions

5.7B1. General rule. Add to the name of a conference, etc. (including that of a conferences entered subordinately, see 5.13), the number of the conference, etc. (if appropriate), the year(s), and the place(s) in which it was held. Separate these elements by a space colon space.

[24.7B1]

5.7B2. Number. If a conference, etc., is stated or inferred to be one of a series of numbered meetings of the same name, add the ordinal numeral in its English form (see AACR 2 Appendix C.8A).

[24.7B2]

> **Conference of British Teachers of Marketing at Advanced Level**
> (*3rd :...*)

If the numbering is irregular, do not add it. *Optionally*, provide an explanation of the irregularities in a note or an explanatory reference.

5.7B3. Date. If the heading is for a single meeting, add the year or years in which the conference, etc., was held.

[24.7B3]

> **Conference on Library Surveys** (*1965 : ...*)
>
> **Conference on Technical Information Center Administration**
> (*3rd : 1966 : ...*)
>
> **Study Institute on Special Education** (*1969-1970 : ...*)

Add specific dates if necessary to distinguish between two or more meetings held in the same year.

> **Conférence agricole interalliée** (*1st : 1919 Feb. 11-15 : ...*)
> **Conférence agricole interalliée** (*2nd : 1919 Mar. 17-19 : ...*)

5.7B4. Location. Add the name of the local place or other location (institution, etc.) in which the conference, etc., was held. Give a local place name in the form prescribed in chapter 4. Give any other location in the nominative case in the language and form in which it is found in the item or material being cataloged.

[24.7B4]

> **Conference on Machinability** (*1965 : London, England*)
>
> **Symposium on Glaucoma** (*1966 : New Orleans, La.*)
>
> **Regional Conference on Mental Measurements of the Blind**
> (*1st : 1951 : Perkins Institution*)
>
> **Louisiana Cancer Conference** (*2nd : 1958 : New Orleans, La.*)
>
> **International Conference on the Biology of Whales**
> (*1971 : Shenandoah National Park*)
>
> **Conference on Cancer Public Education** (*1973 : Dulles Airport*)

If the heading is for a series of conferences, etc., do not add the location unless all were held in the same place.

If the location is part of the name of the conference, etc., do not repeat it.

Arden House Conference on Medicine and Anthropology (*1961*)

Paris Symposium on Radio Astronomy (*1958*)

If the sessions of a conference, etc., were held in two locations, add both names.

World Peace Congress (*1st : 1949 Paris, France, and Prague, Czechoslovakia*)

Institute on Diagnostic Problems in Mental Retardation (*1957 : Long Beach State College and San Francisco State College*)

If the sessions of a conference, etc., were held in three or more locations, add the first named place followed by *etc.*

International Geological Conference (*15th : 1929 : Pretoria, South Africa, etc.*)

5.8. EXHIBITIONS, FAIRS, FESTIVALS, ETC.

5.8A. Omissions
As instructed in 5.7A, omit from the name of an exhibition, fair, festival, etc., word(s) that denote its number.

[24.8A1]

5.8B. Additions
As instructed in 5.7B, add to the name of an exhibition, fair, festival, etc., its number, date, and location. Do not add the location if it is an integral part of the name.

[24.8B]

Festival of Britain (*1951 : London, England*)

Biennale di Venezia (*36th : 1972*)

World's Columbian Exposition (*1893 : Chicago, Ill.*)

Great Exhibition (*1851 : London, England*)

If the year is integrated within the name of the exhibition, etc., and therefore is retained, nevertheless repeat the year as a qualifier.

[RI]

Expo 67 (*1967 : Montréal, Québec*)

5.9. CHAPTERS, BRANCHES, ETC.
If a chapter, branch, etc., entered subordinately (see 5.13), carries out the activities of a corporate body in a particular locality, add the name of the locality, unless it is a part of the name of the chapter, branch, etc.

[24.9A]

Chapters, branches, etc., can normally be recognized in two ways:

a)   the organization is a fraternal one
b)   the designation of every chapter, branch, etc., includes a generic term that is either traditionally used for such (*Post*, *Lodge*, etc.) or an imaginative innovation tending to convey the same sense (*Valley*, *Stake*, etc.).

Consider that the presence of any of these generic designations used for presumably all the chapters, branches, etc., is sufficient reason for subordinate entry in all cases.

[RI]

Freemasons. *Concordia Lodge, No. 13 (Baltimore, Md.)*

Freemasons. *United Grand Lodge (England)*

Knights Templar *(Masonic Order). Grand Commandery (Me.)*

American Legion. *William Peck Post No. 279 (Minneapolis, Minn.)*

Daughters of the American Revolution. *Mary Clap Wooster Chapter (New Haven, Conn.)*

but   **Freemasons.** Minnesota Grand Commandery
(*Name*: Minnesota Grand Commandery)

If the place of activity is an institution, add the name of the institution, unless it is part of the name of the chapter, branch, etc.

Psi Upsilon *(Fraternity).* Gamma Chapter *(Amherst College)*

Society of St. Vincent de Paul. *Conference (Cathedral of St. John the Baptist (Savannah, Ga.))*[8]

5.10. LOCAL CHURCHES, ETC.

5.10A. If the name of a local church, etc., does not convey the idea of a church, etc., add a general designation in English.

[24.10A]

Saint-Nicolas de Donnoso *(Monastery)*

5.10B. Add to the name of a local church, etc., the name of the place or local ecclesiastical jurisdiction in which it is located (see all provisions under 5.4 in choosing the qualifier) unless the location is clear from the name itself.

[24.10B]

Unitarian Universalist Church *(Silver Spring, Md.)*

Saint James' Church *(New York, N.Y.)*

Westover Church *(Charles City County, Va.)*

If the name needs the addition of both a general designation and the name of a place, add the general designation first.

[RI]

Santo Domingo *(Monastery : Pamplona, Spain)*

If there are two or more local churches, etc., with the same name in the same locality, add a further suitable designation.

[24.10B]

Saint James' Church *(New York, N.Y. : Catholic)*

Saint James' Church *(New York, N.Y. : Episcopal)*

---

8. *Conference* is used by this body as the generic word for its local units.

If a church, chapel, etc., is a subordinate unit of a larger institution and is entered directly under its own name (5.12), generally add the name of the larger institution as a qualifier. Make a reference from the name as a subheading of the larger institution. Also make a reference from the place if the body is located in a city or town.

[RI]

> **Chapel of the Good Shepherd** (*General Theological Seminary*)
> *x* General Theological Seminary (New York, N.Y.). Chapel of the Good Shepherd
> *x* New York (N.Y.). Chapel of the Good Shepherd

5.11. RADIO AND TELEVISION STATIONS

5.11A. If the name of a radio or television station consists solely of its call letters or its name does not convey the idea of a radio or television station, add *Radio station* or *Television station* and the name of the place in which the station is located.

[24.11A]

> **WCIA** (*Television station : Champaign, Ill.*)
>
> **WQDR** (*Radio station : Raleigh, N.C.*)

5.11B. Add to the names of any other radio and television station the place in which it is located unless it is an integral part of the name.

[24.11B]

> **Radio Maroc** (*Rabat, Morocco*)
>
> *but*
>
> **Radio London**

Subordinate and Related Bodies

5.12. GENERAL RULE
Enter a subordinate body (other than a government agency entered under jurisdiction, see 5.18) or a related body directly under its own name (see 5.1-5.3) unless its name belongs to one or more of the types listed in 5.13. Refer to the name of a subordinate body entered directly from its name in the form of a subheading of the higher body.

[24.12]

> **Ansco**
> *x* General Aniline and Film Corporation. *Ansco*
>
> **Association of College and Research Libraries**
> *x* American Library Association. *Association of College and Research Libraries*
>
> **BBC Symphony Orchestra**
> *x* British Broadcasting Corporation. *Symphony Orchestra*
>
> **Bodleian Library**
> *x* University of Oxford. *Bodleian Library*
>
> **Congregation of the Most Holy Name of Jesus**
> *x* Dominican Sisters. *Congregation of the Most Holy Name of Jesus*

Crane Theological School
   x Tufts University. *Crane Theological School*

Friends of IBBY
   x International Board on Books for Young People. *Friends*

Harvard Law School
   x Harvard University. *Law School*

5.13. SUBORDINATE AND RELATED BODIES ENTERED SUBORDINATELY

Enter a subordinate or related body as a subheading of the name of the body to which it is subordinate or related if its name belongs to one or more of the following types.[9] Make it a direct or indirect subheading as instructed in 5.14. Omit from the subheading the name or abbreviation of the name of the higher or related body in noun form unless the omission would result in a heading that does not make sense.

[24.13]

[The archival impact of this rule, when taken with the general principle of direct entry (see 5.1), is to limit strictly the use of full hierarchy in corporate name headings. This rule states that a body can be entered subordinately *only* when it falls into one of the six types listed below. A corporate body not meeting these criteria is entered directly under the name by which it is commonly identified. Rule 5.14 further limits the levels of the administrative hierarchy that can be interposed between the name of the body and its parent body. When the heading does not reflect full hierarchy, but this information is important for full understanding of the described material, catalogers should give the information in a note (see 1.7B6) or rely on authority files.]

TYPE 1. A name containing a term that by definition implies that the body is part of another (e.g., *Department, Division, Section, Branch*).[10]

British Broadcasting Corporation. *Engineering Division*

International Federation of Library Associations and Institutions. *Section on Cataloguing*

Stanford University. *Dept. of Civil Engineering*

---

9. Distinguish cases in which the subordinate body's name includes the names of higher bodies from cases in which the names of higher bodies appear only in association with the subordinate body's name.

10. In headings, use the abbreviation *Dept.* for the English word *Department* in the following situations: 1) when the word refers to the name of the body represented by the heading rather than the name of another body, and 2) when the word means a division or section of a larger organization.

Name:	United States Department of Defense
Heading:	**United States.** *Dept. of Defense*
Name:	Task Force on Evaluation of the Department of Defense
Heading:	**United States.** *Task Force on Evaluation of the Department of Defense*
not:	United States. Task Force on Evaluation of the Dept. of Defense

TYPE 2. A name containing a word that normally implies administrative subordination (e.g., *Committee, Commission*, etc.),[11] provided that the name of the higher body is required for the identification of the subordinate body.

Association of State Universities and Land-Grant Colleges. *Committee on Traffic Safety Research and Education*

International Council on Social Welfare. *Canadian Committee*

Timber Trade Federation of the United Kingdom. *Statistical Coordinating Committee*

National Association of Insurance Commissioners. *Securities Valuation Office*

University of Wales. *University Commission*
(*Name*: University Commission)

Society of American Archivists. *National Information Systems Task Force*

but　　**National Commission on United Methodist Higher Education**

TYPE 3. A name that is general in nature or that does no more than indicate a geographic, chronological, or numbered or lettered subdivision of a parent body.

American Dental Association. *Research Institute*
(*Name*: Research Institute)

Bell Telephone Laboratories. *Technical Information Library*
(*Name*: Technical Information Library)

Sondley Reference Library. *Friends of the Library*
(*Name*: Friends of the Library)

---

11. For names of corporate bodies whose official language is English, French, or Spanish, the following words within these entities shall be used to test "administrative subordination":

ENGLISH	FRENCH	SPANISH	
administration	administration	administración	jefatura
administrative ...	agence	agencia	junta
advisory ...	bureau	asesoría	negociado
agency	cabinet	comisaría	oficina
authority	comité	comisión	secretaría
board	commission	comité	secretariado
bureau	délégation	coordinación	servicio
... group	direction	delegación	superintendencia
office	groupe de	disputación	
panel	inspection	dirección	
secretariat	office	directoria	
service	secrétariat	fiscalía	
task force	service	gabinete	
working party	commissariat	gerencia	
	mission	grupo de ...	

American Institute of Architects. *Utah Society*
(*Name*: Utah Society)

Canadian Jewish Congress. *Central Region*
(*Name*: Central Region)

California Home Economics Association. *Orange District*
(*Name*: Orange District)

Dartmouth College. *Class of 1980*
(*Name*: Class of 1980)

International Labour Organisation. *European Regional Conference*
(2nd : 1968 : Geneva, Switzerland)
(*Name*: Second European Regional Conference)

Knights of Labor. *District Assembly 99*
(*Name*: District Assembly 99)

U.S. Customs Service. *Region IX*
(*Name:* Region IX)

TYPE 4. A name that does not convey the idea of a corporate body.

British Library. *Collection Development*
(*Name*: Collection Development)

Bell Canada. *Corporate Public Relations*
(*Name*: Corporate Public Relations

TYPE 5. A name of a university faculty, school, college, institute, laboratory, etc., that simply indicates a particular field of study, interest, or activity.

Princeton University. *Bureau of Urban Research*

Syracuse University. *College of Medicine*

University College London. *Communication Research Centre*

Universität Wien. *Institut für Österreichische Geschichtforschung*

University of California, Berkeley. *University Art Museum*

University of North Carolina at Chapel Hill. *School of Information and Library Science*

University of London. *School of Pharmacy*

TYPE 6. A name that includes the entire name of the higher or related body.

Understand "includes" to apply to any linguistic relationship between the name of the body and its parent (higher or related) body.

Understand "entire name" to apply to the name that was selected for use in the heading for the parent body, not necessarily the catalog-entry form of the parent body's heading (e.g., disregard cataloger's additions to the parent body's name or the fact that the parent body may be entered subordinately). Note, however, that if the heading for the parent body includes a term indicating incorporation, etc. (5.5B1), the form with the term must also appear in the name of the subordinate body for type 6 to be applicable.

[RI]

> **American Legion**. *Auxiliary*
> (*Name*: American Legion Auxiliary)
>
> **Auburn University**. *Agricultural Experiment Station*
> (*Name*: Agricultural Experiment Station of Auburn University)
>
> **Labour Party** (*Great Britain*). *Conference (72nd : 1972 : Blackpool, England)*
> (*Name*: 72nd Annual Conference of the Labour Party)
>
> **United Methodist Church** (*U.S.*). *General Conference*
> (*Name*: General Conference of the United Methodist Church)
>
> **University of Vermont**. *Choral Union*
> (*Name*: University of Vermont Choral Union)
>
> **Yale University**. *Library*
> (*Name*: Yale University Library)

but
> **Hoechst Chemical Society**
> (*Name*: Hoechst Chemical Society)
> (*Name of parent body*: Hoechst A.G.)
>
> **Cambridge University Library**

not
> University of Cambridge. *Library*
> (*Name*: Cambridge University Library)
> (*Name of parent body:* University of Cambridge)
>
> **BBC Symphony Orchestra**

not
> British Broadcasting Company. *Symphony Orchestra*

Exceptions: Treat as falling under type 6 a name that fits one of the following categories:

a)   The subordinate body's name contains the entire name of a directly entered U.S. government body except that one body uses *United States* and the other body uses *U.S.*

b)   The subordinate body's name contains the entire name of its parent body except that the form for the parent body in the subordinate body's name is in another language.

> | | |
> |---|---|
> | *Name of subordinate body*: | South Carolina Advisory Committee to the U.S. Commission on Civil Rights |
> | *Heading for parent body:* | United States Commission on Civil Rights |
> | *Heading for subordinate body:* | **United States Commission on Civil Rights.** *South Carolina Advisory Committee* |

Exclusions from type 6. Type 6 is not applicable to names that fall into the following categories:

a) The name of the subordinate body is made up of the higher body's name plus a designation for the subordinate body that does not by itself convey the idea of a corporate body.

> *Name*: Camden Friends of the Earth
> *Heading*: **Camden Friends of the Earth**
> *not*: Friends of the Earth. Camden

> *Name*: Women of the Minnesota Conference of the United Church of Christ
> *Heading*: **Women of the Minnesota Conference of the United Church of Christ**
> *not*: United Church of Christ. Minnesota Conference. Women

> *Name*: Ladies of the Grand Army of the Republic
> *Heading*: **Ladies of the Grand Army of the Republic**
> *not*: Grand Army of the Republic. Ladies

> *Name*: Saint John's Episcopal Church
> *Heading*: **Saint John's Episcopal Church** (*Knoxville, Tenn.*)
> *not*: Episcopal Church. St. John's (*Knoxville, Tenn.*)

N.B. This category of exclusion does not apply to the subordinate designation *Friends*, as in *Friends of the...*, because this designation has been so commonly used and consequently can be considered "corporate" in connotation.

b) The name of a U.S. state university institution that contains the name of the statewide system.

> *Name*: University of Nebraska Medical Center
> *Heading*: **University of Nebraska Medical Center**
> *not*: University of Nebraska (*Central Administration*). Medical Center

NAMED MEETINGS

If a named meeting contains the entire name of a corporate body (as defined above), enter the meeting subordinately to the heading for the body if the name contains, in addition to the name of the body, no more than a generic term for the meeting, or no more than a generic term plus one or more of the following elements: the venue of the meeting, number, date, or other sequencing events.

> *Name*: Annual Conference of the American Academy of Advertising
> *Heading*: **American Academy of Advertising.** *Conference (22nd : 1980 : University of Missouri-Columbia)*

> *Name*: First Constitutional Convention of the Congress of Industrial Organizations

Heading: **Congress of Industrial Organizations (U.S.).**
Constitutional Convention (1st : 1938 : Pittsburgh, Pa.)

In all other cases, enter a named meeting under its own name.

Name: Unesco International Chemistry Conference
Heading: **Unesco International Chemistry Conference** *(1978 : Perth, W.A.)*

5.14. DIRECT OR INDIRECT SUBHEADING

Enter a body belonging to one or more of the types listed in 5.13 as a subheading of the lowest element in the hierarchy that is entered in its own name. Omit intervening elements in the hierarchy unless the name of the subordinate or related body has been, or is likely to be, used by another body entered under the name of the same higher or related body. In that case, interpose the name of the lowest element in the hierarchy that will distinguish between the bodies.

[24.14A]

Public Library Association. *Audiovisual Committee*
Hierarchy: American Library Association
                 Public Library Association
                 Audiovisual Committee

American Library Association. *Cataloging and Classification Section. Policy and Research Committee*
Hierarchy: American Library Association
                 Resources and Technical Services Division
                 Cataloging and Classification Section
                 Policy and Research Committee

Special Rules

5.15. JOINT COMMITTEES, COMMISSIONS, ETC.

5.15A. Enter a body made up of representatives of two or more other bodies directly under its own name.

[24.15A]

Joint Committee on Individual Efficiency in Industry
(A joint committee of the Department of Scientific and Industrial Research and the Medical Research Council)

Canadian Committee on MARC
(A joint committee of the Association pour l'avancement des sciences et des techniques de la documentation, the Canadian Library Association, and the National Library of Canada)

Omit the names of the parent bodies when these occur within or at the end of the name and if the name of the joint unit is distinctive without them.

Joint Committee on Bathing Places
(*Name*: Joint Committee on Bathing Places of the Conference of State Sanitary Engineers and the Engineering Section of the American Public Health Association)

but **Joint Commission of the Council for Education in World Citizenship and the London International Assembly**

5.15B. If the parent bodies are entered as subheadings of a common higher body, enter the joint unit as a subordinate body as instructed in 5.12-5.14.

[24.15B]

American Library Association. *Joint Committee to Compile a List of International Subscription Agents*
(*A joint committee of the Acquisitions and Serials sections of the American Library Association's Resources and Technical Services Division*)

If a body is composed of representatives of two or more other bodies and these other bodies are all entered as subheadings of a common higher body, enter the joint unit as a subordinate body as instructed in 5.14 or 5.19 if the name of the joint unit fits one of the types under 5.13 or 5.18, respectively.

[RI]

United States. *Joint Meteorological Commission*
x United States. Army. Joint Meteorological Commission
x United States. Navy. Joint Meteorological Commission
x United States. Weather Bureau. Joint Meteorological Commission

5.16. CONVENTIONALIZED SUBHEADINGS FOR STATE AND LOCAL ELEMENTS OF AMERICAN POLITICAL PARTIES

Enter a state or local unit of a political party in the United States under the name of the party followed by the state or local name in parentheses and then the name of the unit. Omit from the name of the unit any indication of the name of the party or the state or locality.

[24.16A]

Republican Party (*Mo.*). *State Committee*
(*Name*: Missouri Republican State Committee)

Republican Party (*Ohio*). *State Executive Committee*
(*Name*: Ohio State Republican State Executive Committee)

Democratic Party (*Tex.*). *State Convention (1857 : Waco, Tex.)*
(*Name*: State Convention of the Democratic Party of the State of Texas)

Government Bodies and Officials

5.17. GENERAL RULE

Enter a body created or controlled by a government under its own name (see 5.1-5.3) unless it belongs to one or more of the types listed in 5.18. However, if a body is subordinate to a higher body that is entered under its own name, formulate the heading for the subordinate body according to 5.12-5.14. Refer to the name of a government agency entered directly from its name in the form of a subheading of the name of the government.

[24.17]

American Battle Monuments Commission
 x United States. *American Battle Monuments Commission*

Arts Council of Great Britain
 x Great Britain. *Arts Council*

Consejo Superior de Investigaciones Científicas
 x Spain. *Consejo Superior de Investigaciones Científicas*

University of British Columbia
 x British Columbia. *University*

5.18. GOVERNMENT AGENCIES ENTERED SUBORDINATELY

Enter a government agency subordinately to the name of the government if it belongs to one or more of the following types. Make it a direct or indirect subheading of the heading for the government as instructed in 5.19. Omit from the subheading the name or abbreviation of the name of the government in noun form unless such an omission would result in a heading that does not make sense.

[24.18A]

> **Canada**. *Information Canada*
> *not*   Canada. *Information*

[The archival impact of this rule, as with 5.13, is to limit strictly the use of administrative hierarchy in headings for government agencies. Again, unless a government agency falls into one of the eleven types enumerated below, it must be entered directly under its own name. For agencies meeting these subordination criteria, rule 5.19 limits the levels of the full hierarchy that may be interposed between the name of an agency and its parent government.]

TYPE 1. An agency with a name containing a term that by definition implies that the body is part of another (e.g., *Department, Division, Section, Branch,* and their equivalents in other languages).

> **Vermont**. *Dept. of Water Resources*
>
> **Ottawa** (*Ont.*). *Dept. of Community Development*
>
> **United States**. *Division of Wildlife Services*

TYPE 2. An agency with a name containing a word that normally implies administrative subordination in the terminology of the government concerned (e.g., *Committee, Commission*),[12] provided that the name of the government is required for the identification of the agency.

---

12. See footnote 11 for terms in English, French, and Spanish to be used to test "administrative subordination."

Australia. *Bureau of Agricultural Economics*

Canada. *Royal Commission on Banking and Finance*

Great Britain. *Central Office of Information*

United States. *Commission on Civil Rights*

United States. *Bureau of Insular Affairs*

but   **Royal Commission on Higher Education in New Brunswick**

TYPE 3. An agency with a name that is general in nature or that does no more than indicate a geographic, chronological, or numbered or lettered subdivision of the government or one of its agencies entered subordinately.

United States. *National Labor Relations Board. Library*
(*Name*: Library)

Niger. *Commissariat général au développement. Centre de documentation*
(*Name*: Centre de documentation)

United States. *General Services Administration. Region 5*
(*Name*: Region 5)

United States. *Public Health Service. Region IX*
(*Name*: Region IX)

Interpretations

National-level bodies. If the body is at the national level of government, consider that the name is "general"--and enter it subordinately--if the name lacks distinctive elements of the following types:

a)   proper nouns or adjectives

    Research Center

    Library

    Technical Laboratory

b)   subject words

c)   the term *National* or *State* (meaning "national") or their equivalents in foreign languages.

Enter the names of all other national level bodies independently.

    Population Research Center

    Nuclear Energy Library

    Technical Laboratory of Oceanographic Research

    National Institutes of Health

    Corporation for Public Broadcasting

    National Gallery

    State Library

Bodies below the national level. If the body is below the national level, and its name does not fall into any other type under 5.18, enter under the heading for the government unless either the name of the government is stated explicitly or is implied in the wording of the name, or the name contains some other element tending to guarantee uniqueness (usually a proper noun or adjective). If variant forms in the body's usage make it unclear as to whether the name includes the name of the government (as defined in the first sentence), do not treat the name of the government as part of the name of the body. In case of doubt as to whether the name of a body below the national level fits the criterion for subordinate entry, enter it subordinately.

Qualifiers. If, according to these instructions, the body is entered under its own name, generally add the name of the government as a qualifier unless this name or an understandable surrogate is already present in the body's name (see 5.4C).

TYPE 4. An agency with a name that does not convey the idea of a corporate body and does not contain the name of a government.

> **Lower Saxony** (*Germany*). *Landesvermessung*
> (*Name*: Landesvermessung)

> **United States**. *Naval Oceanography and Meteorology*
> (*Name*: Naval Oceanography and Meteorology)

> **Canada**. *Ocean and Aquatic Sciences*
> (*Name*: Ocean and Aquatic Sciences)

TYPE 5. An agency that is a ministry or similar major executive agency (i.e., one that has no other agency above it) of a national government as defined by official publications of the government in question.

> **Great Britain**. *Home Office*

> **Great Britain**. *Ministry of Defence*

> **Italy**. *Ministero del bilancio e della programmazione economica*

TYPE 6. A legislative body (see also 5.21).

> **Chicago** (*Ill.*). *City Council*

> **France**. *Assemblée nationale*

> **Great Britain**. *Parliament*

> **United States**. *Congress*

TYPE 7. A court (see also 5.23).

> **Ontario**. *High Court of Justice*

> **United States**. *Supreme Court*

TYPE 8. A principal service of the armed forces of a government (see also 5.24).

> **Canada**. *Canadian Armed Forces*

Germany. *Heer*

Great Britain. *Army*

United States. *Navy*

TYPE 9. A head of state or head of government (see also 5.20).

Great Britain. *Sovereign*

Montréal (*Québec*). *Mayor*

United States. *President*

Virginia. *Governor*

TYPE 10. An embassy, consulate, etc. (see also 5.25).

Canada. *Embassy (U.S.)*

Great Britain. *Consulate (New York, N.Y.)*

TYPE 11. A delegation to an international or intergovernmental body (see also 5.26).

Great Britain. *Delegation to the United Nations*

5.19. DIRECT OR INDIRECT SUBHEADING

Enter an agency belonging to one or more of the types listed in 5.18 as a direct subheading of the heading for the government unless the name of the agency has been, or is likely to be, used by another agency entered under the name of the same government. In that case, interpose between the name of the government and the name of the agency, the name of the lowest element in the hierarchy that will distinguish between the agencies.

[24.19A]

[See commentary under 5.18]

United States. *Office of Human Development Services*
  Hierarchy: United States
        Department of Health, Education and Welfare
        Office of Human Development Services

Québec (*Province*). *Service de l'exploration géologique*
  Hierarchy: Québec
        Ministère des richesses naturelles
        Direction générale des mines
        Direction de géologie
        Service de l'exploration géologique

United States. *Aviation Forecast Branch*
  Hierarchy: United States
        Department of Transportation
        Federal Aviation Administration
        Office of Aviation Policy
        Aviation Forecast Branch

France. *Commission centrale des marchés*
    Hierarchy: France
                    Ministère de l'économie et des finances
                    Commission centrale des marchés

but

Great Britain. *Dept. of Employment. Solicitor's Office*
    Hierarchy: Great Britain
                    Department of Employment
                    Solicitor's Office
(*Other ministries and departments have had subordinate units called* Solicitor's Office)

France. *Direction général des impôts. Service de l'administration général*
    Hierarchy: France
                    Ministère de l'économie et des finances
                    Direction général des impôts
                    Service de l'administration général
(*Other units within the same ministry are called* Service de l'administration générale)

Special Rules

5.20. GOVERNMENT OFFICIALS

5.20A. Scope
Apply this rule only to officials of countries and other states that have existed in postmedieval times, and to officials of international intergovernmental organizations.

[24.20A1]

5.20B. Heads of state, etc.
Enter a sovereign, president, other head of state, or governor acting in an official capacity under the heading for the jurisdiction, followed by the title of the official in English (unless there is no equivalent English term). Add the inclusive years of the reign or incumbency and the name of the person in a brief form and in the language of the heading for that person.

[24.20B1]

United States. *President (1953-1961 : Eisenhower)*

Illinois. *Governor (1973-1977 : Walker)*

Papal States. *Sovereign (1846-1870 : Pius IX)*

If the title varies with the sex of the incumbent, use a general term (e.g., *Sovereign* rather than *King* or *Queen*).

Great Britain. *Sovereign (1952-   : Elizabeth II)*

Russia. *Sovereign (1894-1917 : Nicholas II)*

Spain. *Sovereign (1886-1931 : Alfonso XIII)*

If there are two or more nonconsecutive periods of incumbency, use separate headings.

United States. *President (1885-1889 : Cleveland)*

United States. *President (1893-1897 : Cleveland)*

If the heading applies to more than one incumbent, do not add the dates and names.

United States. *President*

5.20C. Heads of governments and of international intergovernmental bodies

5.20C1. Enter a head of government acting in an official capacity who is not also a head of state under the heading for the jurisdiction, followed by the title of the official in the vernacular. Do not add dates or names.

[24.20C1]

Great Britain. *Prime Minister*

Philadelphia *(Pa.). Mayor*

France. *Premier ministre*

Italy. *Presidente del Consiglio dei ministri*

5.20C2. Enter a head of an international intergovernmental organization acting in an official capacity under the heading for the organization, followed by the title of the official in the language of the heading for the organization.

[24.20C2]

United Nations. *Secretary-General*

5.20D. Governors of dependent or occupied territories

Enter a governor of a dependent territory (e.g., colony, protectorate, etc.), or of an occupied territory (see 5.6D) acting in an official capacity under the heading for the colony, territory, etc., followed by the title of the governor in the language of the governing power.

[24.20D1]

Falkland Islands. *Governor*

Jersey *(Channel Islands) (Territory under German occupation, 1940-1945). Militärischer Befehlshaber*

Netherlands. *(Territory under German occupation, 1940-1945). Reichskommisar für die Besetzten Niederländischen Gebiete*

Germany *(Territory under Allied occupation, 1945-1955 : U.S. Zone). Military Governor*

5.20E. Other officials

Enter any other official under the heading for the ministry or agency that the official represents.

[24.20E1]

        United States. *General Accounting Office*
not   United States. *Comptroller General*

        United States. *Dept. of State*
not   United States. *Secretary of State*

Minnesota. *Dept. of Administration*
not   Minnesota. *Commissioner of Administration*

Enter an official who is not part of a ministry, etc., or who is part of a ministry, etc., that is identified only by the title of the official, under the heading for the jurisdiction, followed by the title of the official.

[24.20E2]

Great Britain. *Lord Privy Seal*

Alabama. *Secretary of State*

5.21. LEGISLATIVE BODIES

5.21A. Enter a legislature under the name of the jurisdiction for which it legislates.

[24.21A]

Iceland. *Althing*

If a legislature has more than one chamber, enter each as a subheading for the legislature.

Great Britain. *Parliament. House of Commons*
not   Great Britain. *House of Commons*

United States. *Congress. Senate*
not   United States. *Senate*

Colorado. *General Assembly. House of Representatives*
not   Colorado. House of Representatives

5.21B. Enter a committee or other subordinate unit (other than a legislative subcommittee of the United States Congress, see 5.21C) as a subheading of the legislature or of a particular chamber, as appropriate.[13]

[24.21B]

United States. *Congress. Joint Committee on the Library*

United States. *Congress. House. Select Committee on Government Organization*

Minnesota. *Legislature. Senate. Committee on Education*

New York *(State). Legislature. Assembly. Committee on Canals*

Florida. *Legislature. House of Representatives. Committee on Youth*

5.21C. Enter a legislative subcommittee of the United States Congress as a subheading of the committee to which it is subordinate. Apply this rule also to legislative subcommittees of the U.S. states.

[24.21C]

United States. *Congress. Senate. Committee on Foreign Relations. Subcommittee on Canadian Affairs*
not   United States. *Congress. Senate. Subcommittee on Canadian Affairs*

---

13. According to Library of Congress rule interpretations, *House* is considered the conventional name of the United States House of Representatives. This does not apply to *state* houses of representatives.

> **Illinois.** *General Assembly. House of Representatives. Select Committee on Aeronautics. Subcommittee on Aviation Transportation Safety*

not   Illinois. General Assembly. House of Representatives. Subcommittee on Aviation Transportation Safety

5.21D. If successive legislatures are numbered consecutively, add the ordinal number and the year or years to the heading for the particular legislature or one of its chambers.

[24.21D]

> **United States.** *Congress (87th : 1961-1962)*
>
> **United States.** *Congress (87th : 1961-1962). House*

If, in such a case, numbered sessions are involved, add the session and its number and the year or years of the session to the number of the legislature.

> **United States.** *Congress (87th, 2nd session : 1962)*
>
> **United States.** *Congress (87th, 2nd session : 1962). House*

5.22. CONSTITUTIONAL CONVENTIONS

5.22A. Enter a constitutional convention under the heading for the government that convened it, followed by the name of the convention. Add the year or years in which it was held.

[24.22A]

> **Germany.** *Nationalversammlung (1919-1920)*
>
> **Portugal.** *Assembleia Nacional Constituinte (1911)*

5.22B. If there is a variation in the forms of name of constitutional conventions convened by a jurisdiction using English as an official language, use *Constitutional Convention* as the subheading for each of the conventions.

[24.22B]

> **New Hampshire.** *Constitutional Convention (1781)*

not   New Hampshire. *Convention for Framing a New Constitution or Form of Government (1781)*

> **New Hampshire.** *Constitutional Convention (1889)*
>
> **New Hampshire.** *Constitutional Convention (1912)*

not   New Hampshire. *Convention to Revise the Constitution (1912)*

If English is not an official language of the jurisdiction, follow the instructions in 5.2 and 5.3.

5.23. COURTS

5.23A. Civil and criminal courts
Enter a civil or criminal court under the heading for the jurisdiction whose authority it exercises, followed by the name of the court.

[24.23A1]

> **Vermont.** *Court of Chancery*

Omit the name (or abbreviation of the name) of the place in which the court sits or the area which it serves unless the omission would result in objectionable distortion. If the name of the place or area served is required to distinguish a court from others of the same name, add it in a conventionalized form.

> **France**. *Cour d'appel (Caen)*
> (*Name*: Cour d'appel de Caen)

> **Great Britain**. *Crown Court (Manchester)*
> (*Name*: Manchester Crown Court)

> **United States**. *Court of Appeals (2nd Circuit)*
> (*Name*: United States Court of Appeals for the Second Circuit)

> **United States**. *Court of Appeals (District of Columbia Circuit)*
> (*Name*: United States Court of Appeals for the District of Columbia Circuit)

> **United States**. *District Court (Delaware)*
> (*Name*: United States District Court for the District of Delaware)

> **United States**. *District Court (North Carolina : Eastern District)*
> (*Name*: United States District Court for the Eastern District of North Carolina)

> **United States**. *District Court (Illinois : Northern District : Eastern Division)*
> (*Name*: United States District Court for the Eastern Division of the Northern District of Illinois)

> **California**. *Municipal Court (Los Angeles Judicial District)*
> (*Name*: Municipal Court, Los Angeles Judicial District)

> **California**. *Superior Court (San Bernadino County)*
> (*Name*: Superior Court for the State of California in and for the County of San Bernadino)

> **Texas**. *County Court (Calhoun County)*
> (*Name*: County Court of Calhoun County)

In formulating headings for prosecuting attorneys of jurisdictions, apply the principle of conventionalized heading used in 5.23 for the heading for the court with which the attorneys are closely associated.

a) Enter under the heading for the appropriate jurisdiction. Note that in the states of the United States prosecuting attorneys are agents of the state as a whole, not agents of a particular county.
b) Use a conventionalized name for the office (e.g., *Attorney, District Attorney*).
c) Add as a parenthetical qualifier the name of the particular area served.

[RI]

> **United States**. *Attorney (District of Columbia)*

> **United States**. *Attorney (Illinois : Northern District)*

> **New Mexico**. *District Attorney (2nd Judicial District)*

> **Wisconsin**. *District Attorney (Milwaukee County)*

5.23B. Ad hoc military courts

Enter an ad hoc military court (e.g., court-martial, court of inquiry) under the heading for the particular military service, followed by the name of the court. Add the surname of the defendant and the year of the trial.

[24.23B]

United States. *Army. Court of Inquiry (Hall : 1863)*

Virginia. *Militia. Court-martial (Yancey : 1806)*

5.24. ARMED FORCES

5.24A. Armed forces at the national level

Enter a principal service of the armed forces of a national government under the heading for the government, followed by the name of the service. Omit the name (or abbreviation of the name) of the government in noun form unless the omission would result in objectionable distortion.

[24.24A1]

Canada. *Canadian Armed Forces*

Great Britain. *Royal Navy*

United States. *Marine Corps*[14]

Great Britain. *Royal Marines*[14]

Enter a component branch, command district, or military unit,[15] large or small, as a direct subheading of the heading for the principal service of which it is a part.

Great Britain. *Army. Royal Gloucestershire Hussars*

---

14. The Marine Corps and the Royal Marines are treated as principal services.

15. Define "component branch, command district, or military unit" as an agency that constitutes:
1) A unit subject to combat service or an administrative unit over such units, e.g.,
      commands
      corps
      fleets
      general staffs
      military districts
      regiments or divisions of infantry, etc.
2) A unit that serves as a direct support unit to category 1, e.g.,
      corps of engineers
      legal units, e.g., judge advocate general
      material command
      medical corps
      military police
      transport service
   This means treating the following types of bodies under general rules:
      research agencies, e.g., laboratories, research centers, institutes, experiment stations, museums
      schools, e.g. service academies, Air University
      musical groups, e.g., military bands, choirs, etc.
      armories, arsenals
      base hospitals, other hospitals
   Treat forts, bases, camps, airfields, etc., as jurisdictions (see 4.1).

Great Britain. *Royal Air Force. Central Interpretation Unit*

Great Britain. *Royal Navy. Sea Cadet Corps*

United States. *Army. General Staff*

United States. *Army. Corps of Engineers*

United States. *Army. Far East Command*

United States. *Army. District of Mindanao*

If the component branch, etc., is identified by a number, follow the style of numbering found in the name (spelled out, roman numerals, or arabic numerals) and place the numbering after the name.

Great Britain. *Army. Infantry Regiment, 57th*

France. *Armée. Régiment de dragons, 15ᵉ*

Germany. *Heer. Panzerdivision, 11*

Exception: If a component branch of a *United States* military service is identified by a number, use arabic ordinal numerals in the heading and place the numerals after the name. If the form of the numbering found on the item being cataloged differs from the form used in the heading, make a reference from the form found, in the order that matches the heading.

[RI]

United States. *Army. Infantry Division, 27th*

United States. *Navy. Fleet, 6th*
    x United States. *Navy. Fleet, Sixth*

United States. *Army. Army, 1st*
    x United States. *Army, First*

United States. *Army. Corps, 4th*
    x United States. *Army. Corps, IV*

United States. *Army. Engineer Combat Battalion, 2nd*

United States. *Army. Volunteer Cavalry, 1st*

United States. *Navy. Torpedo Squadron, 8th*
    x United States. *Navy. Torpedo Squadron 8*

If the name of such a component branch, etc., begins with the name, or an indication of the name, of the principal service, enter it as a direct subheading of the heading for the government.

[24.24A1]

United States. *Army Map Service*

United States. *Naval Air Transport Service*

If the name of such a component branch, etc., contains but does not begin with the name or an indication of the name of the principal service, enter it as a direct subheading of the heading for the service and omit the name or indication of the name unless objectionable distortion would result.

Canada. *Canadian Army. Royal Canadian Army Medical Corps*

U.S. Civil War Units. When establishing either Union or Confederate fighting units of the U.S. Civil War consult reference works[16] to determine the essential information needed to construct the heading. Since many Civil War units are often known by popular or colloquial names, use conventionalized forms of headings as subheadings of either the United States or the Confederate States of America.

If the unit is one of a numbered sequence, use arabic ordinal numbers in the heading for each unit in the sequence. Make references from the standardized form beginning with the state name.

N.B. Because of the high incidence of conflicts for Union units, a date qualifier (for the duration of the unit) is added routinely. Normally, there is no such problem of conflict with Confederate units.

[RI]

UNION UNITS

> **United States.** *Army. Ohio Infantry Regiment, 42nd (1861-1864)*
> (*Name*: 42nd Regiment of Ohio Volunteers)
> *x* Ohio Infantry. *42nd Regiment (1861-1864)*

> **United States.** *Army. Ohio Infantry Regiment, 48th (1861-1865)*
> (*Name*: Forty-eighth Ohio Veteran Volunteer Infantry)
> *x* Ohio Infantry. *48th Regiment (1861-1865)*

> **United States.** *Army. Pennsylvania Cavalry Regiment, 6th (1861-1865)*
> (*Name*: Sixth Pennsylvania Cavalry)
> *x* Pennsylvania Cavalry. *6th Regiment (1861-1865)*

> **United States.** *Army. Pennsylvania Cavalry Regiment, 7th (1861-1865)*
> (*Name*: Seventh Pennsylvania Veteran Volunteer Cavalry)
> *x* Pennsylvania Cavalry. *7th Regiment (1861-1865)*

CONFEDERATE UNITS

> **Confederate States of America.** *Army. Tennessee Infantry Regiment, 19th*
> (*Name*: Old Nineteenth Tennessee Regiment, C.S.A.)
> *x* Tennessee Infantry. *19th Regiment*

> **Confederate States of America.** *Army. Alabama Infantry Regiment, 1st*
> (*Name*: First Regiment, Alabama Volunteer Infantry, C.S.A.)
> *x* Alabama Infantry. *1st Regiment*

---

16. Such reference works include *The Union Army* (Madison, Wis.: Federal Pub. Co., 1908); *Official Army Register of the Volunteer Force of the U.S. Army for the Years 1861-1865* (Washington, D.C: Adjutant General's Office, 1865-1867); William Frayne Amann, ed., *Personnel of the Civil War*, v. 1, Confederate; v. 2, Union (New York, N.Y.: T. Yoseloff, 1961); and W. J. Tancig, *Confederate Military Land Units, 1861-1865* (South Brunswick, N.J.: T. Yoseloff, 1967).

5.24B. Armed forces below the national level

Enter an armed force of a government below the national level under the heading for the government followed by the name of the force.

[24.24B1]

> **New York** *(State). Militia*
>
> **New York** *(State). National Guard*

Enter a component branch of an armed force below the national level as a subheading of the heading for the force as instructed in 5.24A.

[24.24B2]

> **New York** *(State). Militia. Regiment of Artillery, 9th*
> (*Name*: 9th Regiment of Artillery, N.Y.S.M.)
>
> **New York** *(State). National Guard. Coast Defense Command, 9th*

Enter a component branch, etc., of a force below the national level that has been absorbed into the national military forces as a component branch of the national force (see 5.24A; see also instructions for U.S. Civil War units).

[24.24B3]

5.25. EMBASSIES, CONSULATES, ETC.

Enter an embassy, consulate, legation, or other continuing office representing one country in another under the heading for the country represented, followed by the name of the embassy, etc. Give the subheading in the language (see 5.3A) of the country represented, and omit it from the name of the country.

If the heading is for an embassy or legation, add the name of the country to which it is accredited.

[24.25A]

> **Germany.** *Gesandtschaft (Switzerland)*
>
> **Great Britain.** *Embassy (U.S.)*
>
> **United States.** *Legation (Bulgaria)*
>
> **Yugoslavia.** *Poslantsvo (U.S.)*
>
> **Canada.** *Embassy (Belgium)*

If the heading is for a consulate or other local office, add the name of the city in which it is located.

> **France.** *Consulat (Buenos Aires, Argentina)*
>
> **Great Britain.** *Consulate (Cairo, Egypt)*

5.26. DELEGATIONS TO INTERNATIONAL AND INTERGOVERNMENTAL BODIES

Enter a delegation, commission, etc., representing a country in an international or intergovernmental body, conference, undertaking, etc., under the heading for the country represented, followed by the name of the delegation, etc. Give the subheading in the language (see 5.3A) of the country represented. Omit from the subheading the name or abbreviation of the name of the government in noun form unless such an omission would result in objectionable distortion. If the name of the delegation, etc., is uncertain, give *Delegation* [*Mission*, etc.] *to...* (or equivalent terms in the language of the country represented). Omit number, date, and location statements found in the name of a delegation, etc., to a meeting, and add the number, date, and location (in that order) at the end of the heading (see 5.7B).

[24.26A]

> **United States**. *Mission to the United Nations*
>
> **United States**. *Delegation to the General Assembly of the United Nations*
>
> **Uruguay**. *Delegación en las Naciones Unidas*

When the delegation is to a meeting, add number, date, and place of the meeting in a conventionalized manner to the end of the heading according to 5.7. Use a sequence of commas to connect the data elements, i.e., do not treat these elements as AACR 2 qualifiers but as part of the cataloger's construction of the name.

[RI]

> **Mexico**. *Delegación a la Conferencia Interamericana de Consolidación de la Paz, 1936, Buenos Aires*
>
> **Germany**. *Reichskommission für die Weltausstellung in Chicago, 1893*
>
> **Ecuador**. *Segunda Delegación a la Conferencia Panamericana de Bellas Artes, 5th, 1949, Lima, Peru*

If it is uncertain that a delegation represents the government of a country, enter it under its own name.

[24.26A]

Religious Bodies and Officials

5.27. RELIGIOUS BODIES AND OFFICIALS

5.27A. Councils, etc., of a single religious body

5.27A1. Enter a council, etc., of the clergy and/or membership (international, national, regional, provincial, state, or local) of a single religious body under the heading for the religious body, followed by the name of the council, etc. When appropriate, make additions to the heading as instructed in 5.7B.

[24.27A1]

> **Catholic Church**. *Antilles Episcopal Conference*
>
> **Society of Friends**. *Philadelphia Yearly Meeting*[17]

5.27A2. If the name of a council, etc., of the Catholic Church is given in more than one language, use (in this order of preference) the English, Latin, French, German, or Spanish name, and make appropriate references.

[24.27A2]

> **Catholic Church**. *Canadian Conference of Catholic Bishops*
>
> **Catholic Church**. *Concilium Plenarium Americae Latinae* (*1899 : Rome, Italy*)

---

17. *Yearly Meeting* is used by the Society of Friends to denote a particular level in its structure.

> **Catholic Church.** *Plenary Council of Baltimore (2nd : 1866)*
>   *x* Catholic Church. *Concilium Plenarium Baltimorensis (2nd : 1866)*

5.27A3. If a council, etc., is subordinate to a particular district of the religious body, enter it under the heading for that district (see 5.27C2-5.27C3), followed by the name of the council, etc. If the name appears in more than one language, use the name in the vernacular of the district.

[24.27A3]

> **Catholic Church.** *Province of Baltimore. Provincial Council (10th : 1869)*
>
> **Catholic Church.** *Province of Mexico City. Concilio Provincial (3rd : 1585)*

5.27B. Religious officials

5.27B1. Enter a religious official (e.g., bishop, abbot, rabbi, moderator, mullah, patriarch) acting in an official capacity under the heading for the religious jurisdiction (e.g., diocese, order, rabbinate, synod, denomination, see 5.27C2-5.27C3), followed by the title of the official in English (unless there is no equivalent English term). Add the inclusive years of incumbency and the name of the person in a brief form and in the language of the heading for that person.

[24.27B1]

> **Catholic Church.** *Diocese of Campos. Bishop (1949-1981: Mayer)*
>
> **Franciscans.** *Minister General (1947-1951 : Perantoni)*
>
> **Catholic Church.** *Diocese of Winchester. Bishop (1367-1404 : William, of Wykeham)*

If the heading applies to more than one incumbent, do not add the dates and names.

> **Church of England.** *Diocese of Winchester. Bishop*

5.27B2. Popes. Enter a pope acting in an official capacity under *Catholic Church*, followed by *Pope*. Add the year or inclusive years of the reign, and the pontifical name in its catalog entry form (see 3.13B).

[24.27B2]

> **Catholic Church.** *Pope (1878-1903 : Leo XIII)*
>
> **Catholic Church.** *Pope (1978 : John Paul I)*

If the heading applies to more than one pope, do not add the dates and names.

> **Catholic Church.** *Pope*

5.27C. Subordinate bodies

5.27C1. General rule. Except as provided in 5.27C2-5.27C4, enter subordinate religious bodies according to the instructions in 5.12-5.13. For religious orders and societies, see 5.3D.

[24.27C1]

5.27C2. Provinces, dioceses, synods, etc. Enter a province, diocese, synod, or other subordinate unit of a religious body having jurisdiction over a geographic area under the heading for the religious body, followed by the name of the province, etc.

[24.27C2]

Church of England. *Diocese of Ely*

Evangelical and Reformed Church. *Reading Synod*

Evangelische Kirche der Altpreussischen Union. *Kirchenprovinz Sachsen*

Church of England. *Archdeaconry of Surrey*

Episcopal Church. *Diocese of Southern Virginia*

Church of England. *Woking Deanery*

United Methodist Church *(U.S.). Northern Illinois Conference*

5.27C3. Catholic dioceses, etc. Use an English form of name for a patriarchate, diocese, province, etc., of the Catholic Church. Give the name of the see according to the instructions in chapter 4. If the name of the see itself, as given, would be a heading and this heading would include a larger geographic qualifier, then add the qualifier within parentheses.

[24.27C3; RI]

Catholic Church. *Archdiocese of Santiago de Cuba*

Catholic Church. *Diocese of Ely (England)*

Do not apply this rule to an ecclesiastical principality (often called *Bistum*) of the Holy Roman Empire bearing the same name as a Catholic diocese and ruled by the same bishop.

[24.27C3]

Catholic Church. *Diocese of Fulda*

but

Fulda *(Ecclesiastical principality)*

5.27C4. Central administrative organs of the Catholic Church (Roman Curia)

Enter a congregation, tribunal, or other central administrative organ (i.e., one that is part of the Roman Curia) of the Catholic Church under *Catholic Church*, followed by the Latin form of the name of the congregation, etc. Omit any form of the word *sacer* when it is the first word of the name.

[24.27C4]

Catholic Church. *Congregatio Sacrorum Rituum*

Catholic Church. *Congregatio de Propaganda Fide*

Catholic Church. *Rota Romana*

5.27D. Papal diplomatic missions, etc.

Enter a diplomatic mission from the pope to a secular power under *Catholic Church*, followed by *Apostolic Nunciature* or *Apostolic Internunciature*, as appropriate. Add the heading for the government to which the mission is accredited.

[24.27D1]

Catholic Church. *Apostolic Internunciature (India)*

Catholic Church. *Apostolic Nunciature (Flanders)*

Enter a nondiplomatic apostolic delegation under *Catholic Church* followed by *Apostolic Delegation*. Add the name of the country or other jurisdiction in which the delegation functions.

Catholic Church. *Apostolic Delegation (France)*

Enter an emissary of the pope acting in an official capacity (other than a nuncio, internuncio, or apostolic delegate) under *Catholic Church*, followed by the title of the emissary (in English if there is an equivalent term; otherwise in Latin). Add the name of the country or region in which the emissary functions.

Catholic Church. *Legate (Colombia)*

If the country or region is not ascertained, add the name of the emissary in brief form.

Catholic Church. *Commissary Apostolic (Robertus Castellensis)*

CHAPTER 6

UNIFORM TITLES

Contents

INTRODUCTION

Chapter 25 of AACR 2 deals with a concept in library cataloging known as *uniform title*. The word *uniform* designates the species of access points or headings that are formulated by the cataloger in a uniform manner rather than transcribed from the physical items. A uniform title provides the means for bringing together all catalog entries for a *work* when various manifestations (e.g., editions, translations) of it have appeared under various titles.

A body of archival material, however, seldom appears "in various manifestations ... under various titles," and a cataloger routinely is required to *supply* (i.e., construct) a title when the body of material lacks a formal title. Thus, archival catalogers will use uniform titles primarily in creating secondary (added) entries or subject headings, and in cataloging manuscript versions of works that *have* appeared in various manifestations.

In the examples below the uniform title *Martin Chuzzlewit* was constructed by the cataloger to bring together variously titled editions (which could include manuscript versions) of that work.[1]

> **Dickens, Charles**, 1812-1870
> [Martin Chuzzlewit] (*Uniform title*)
> The life and adventures of Martin Chuzzlewit
> (*Title on physical item*)

> **Dickens, Charles**, 1812-1870
> [Martin Chuzzlewit] (*Uniform title*)
> Martin Chuzzlewit's life and adventures
> (*Title on physical item*)

A uniform title alone (i.e., with no associated personal or corporate name main entry) may constitute the main entry or secondary entry heading for a work. This is true for such works as sacred scriptures, anonymous classics, and certain manuscripts.

> **Bible ...**

> **Chanson de Roland**

> **Domesday book**

A uniform title is also used in association with a personal or corporate name heading, where appropriate, to form a *name-title* heading, frequently required for secondary (added) entries or subject headings.

> **Dickens, Charles, 1812-1870. Martin Chuzzlewit**

In constructing a name-title heading for a body of archival materials (to use either for secondary entries or subject headings), the cataloger uses the personal or corporate name main entry (if applicable) and the title that would appear in a bibliographic record for the materials.

Bibliographic record for body of archival materials:

> **Neill, Edward D. (Edward Duffield), 1823-1893.**
> Papers, 1768-1931.

Added entry or subject heading used in another bibliographic record:

> **Neill, Edward D. (Edward Duffield), 1823-1893. Papers, 1768-1931**

Bibliographic record for body of archival materials:

> **Harkness collection, 1525-1651.**

Added entry or subject heading used in another bibliographic record:

> **Harkness collection, 1525-1651.**

---

1. A title that appears as an item title in one instance may appear as a uniform title in another. For example, *Martin Chuzzlewit* may have appeared as an actual publication title. In the USMARC format it is possible to differentiate between the two: if *Martin Chuzzlewit* is the transcribed publication title in the particular record it is tagged 245; if it is a uniform title it is tagged 240. For a uniform title that stands alone as the entire heading, such as *Bible*, the tag is 130.

This chapter contains instructions for the most common applications of uniform title headings in archival cataloging. There is much less direct incorporation from the AACR 2 rules than in chapters 3-5. As with all other material in this manual that is derived from or dependent on AACR 2, any special questions or problems should be resolved by consulting AACR 2.

6.1. GENERAL RULE

When cataloging any individual archival item or manuscript of a work that is subject to the application of uniform titles, follow the rules given in chapter 25 of AACR 2. This would include most particularly literary works that have appeared in various manifestations, editions, translations, etc.; sacred scriptures; liturgical works; laws; treaties; and musical works.

Enclose a uniform title in square brackets, and give it before the title proper (see introductory examples). If the work is entered under title, give the uniform title as the heading with square brackets. *Optionally*, record a uniform title used as a main entry heading without square brackets.

6.2. ADDITIONS TO UNIFORM TITLES

Add in parentheses an appropriate explanatory word, brief phrase, or other designation to distinguish a uniform title used as a heading from an identical or similar heading.

[25.5B1]

Sayers, Dorothy L. (Dorothy Leigh), 1893-1957. Busman's honeymoon (*Novel*)

Sayers, Dorothy L. (Dorothy Leigh), 1893-1957. Busman's honeymoon (*Play*)
(*Two separate works with the same title by the same person*)

6.3. UNIFORM TITLES IN SECONDARY ENTRIES

This rule applies when an added entry or subject heading is required to represent a literary or other work.[2]

For a work that would be entered under title alone, use the uniform title alone.

Analecta anglicana
(*For titled work of unknown authorship*)

For a work that would be entered under a person or corporate body, use a uniform title under a name heading.

Kennedy, John F. (John Fitzgerald), 1917-1963. Profiles in courage

Whitman, Walt, 1819-1892. Leaves of grass

Minnesota Library Association. Records, 1891-1977

6.4. RADIO AND TELEVISION PROGRAMS

This rule applies to main entries, added entries, or subject headings.

For a specific radio or television program, use a uniform title heading, modified by the phrase (*Radio program*) or (*Television program*) as appropriate. Omit initial articles

---

2. A body of archival material may be thought of as a "work" of accumulation.

and make other appropriate additions to distinguish among different works with the same title proper.

> **Amos 'n' Andy** (*Radio program*)
>
> **Mary Tyler Moore show** (*Television program*)
>
> **Lux summer theater** (*Radio program*)
>
> **Dragnet** (*Television program : 1952-1959*)
>
> **Dragnet** (*Television program : 1967-1970*)

6.5. NEWSPAPER AND PERIODICAL TITLES

When making an added entry or subject heading for a newspaper, etc., use the title[3] or (less frequently) name heading and title as they would appear on the item's own bibliographic record. In formulating such headings, follow the rules of capitalization and punctuation for titles (see 1.1B1).[4]

> **New York times** (*New York, N.Y. : 1857*)
>
> **Library of Congress. Annual report of the Librarian of Congress for the fiscal year ended 1988**
>
> **Saturday review** (*New York, N.Y. : 1975*)
>
> **MLA newsletter** (*Minnesota Library Association*)
>
> **Advances in library automation and networking**

6.6. COMICS

Comic strips by one person as works of personal authorship are represented by name-title headings. If there is a need to differentiate between the comic strip as a whole and a book of selections from it carrying the same title as the strip, add an appropriate parenthetical qualifier.

[RI]

> **Trudeau, G. B., 1948- Doonesbury**
>
> **Trudeau, G. B., 1948- Doonesbury** (*Comic strip*)
>
> **Blondie** (*Comic strip*)

6.7. MOTION PICTURES

Use a uniform title heading for a motion picture title used as an added entry or subject heading. Add the qualifier *Motion picture* to the title.

[RI]

> **M*A*S*H** (*Motion picture*)
>
> **Miracle on 34th Street** (*Motion picture : 1947*)
>
> **Miracle on 34th Street** (*Motion picture : 1973*)

---

3. A newspaper, periodical, serial publication, etc., is most frequently entered under its title according to rules in chapter 21 of AACR 2.

4. A bibliographic record for the *records* of a newspaper, etc., generally would be entered under the heading for corporate body responsible for the intellectual content of the materials, probably the publisher (see especially 2.1B2 and 5.1).
> **New York Times** (Firm).
> Records, 1857-1986.

6.8. COMPUTER PROGRAMS

Add the qualifier *Computer program* to the title of a computer program used as a secondary entry.

[RI]

dBase III plus (*Computer program*)

Microsoft Flight simulator (*Computer program*)

6.9. MANUSCRIPTS AND MANUSCRIPT GROUPS

6.9A. Scope

Use this rule:

a) to formulate a uniform title for a work contained in a manuscript or manuscripts (including manuscript groups) when the preceding rules in this chapter do not provide a uniform title

b) to formulate a heading for a manuscript or manuscripts (including manuscript groups) when the item being cataloged merits an added entry for the manuscript(s).

[25.13A1]

6.9B. General rule

Use as the uniform title for a work contained in manuscript(s), or for a manuscript itself or for a manuscript group (in this order or preference):

[25.13B1]

a) a title that has been assigned to the work subsequent to its creation or compilation

Domesday book

Godwulf manuscript

b) the name of the manuscript(s) if the work is identified only by that name

Book of Lismore

Dead Sea scrolls

Tell el-Amarna tablets

c) the heading (see chapter 5) of the repository followed by *Manuscript* and the repository's designation for the manuscript(s). If the item being cataloged is a single manuscript within a collection, add the foliation if known.

British Library. Manuscript. Arundel 384

British Library. Manuscript. Additional 15233, fol. 11-27

If the uniform title is chosen by the application of a) or b) above and the item has a repository designation, refer from that designation.

Codex Brucianus
x Bodleian Library. Manuscript. Bruce 96

6.10. LEGAL MATERIALS

6.10A. Collections. Use *Laws, etc.* for a complete or partial collection of legislative enactments of a jurisdiction, other than a compilation on a particular subject.[5]

[25.15A1]

> **Great Britain**
> [Laws, etc.]
> Halsbury's statutes of England...

> **United States**
> [Laws, etc.]
> United States code...

> **Ontario**
> [Laws, etc.]
> Statutes of the Province of Ontario passed in the session held at Toronto in the twenty-third and twenty-fourth years of the reign of Her Majesty Queen Elizabeth II...

> **Boston** (*Mass.*)
> [Laws, etc.]
> The revised ordinances of 1961 of the city of Boston

If a compilation of laws on a particular subject has a citation title, use that.

> **California**
> [Agricultural code]
> West's California agricultural code

> **Great Britain**
> [Licensing acts]
> Paterson's licensing acts

6.10B. Single laws, etc. Use as the uniform title for a single legislative enactment (in this order of preference):

a)   the official short title or citation title
b)   the unofficial short title or citation title used in legal literature
c)   the official title of the enactment
d)   any other official designation (e.g., the number or date)

[25.15A2]

> **Great Britain**
> [Field Monuments Act 1972]

> **New Zealand**
> [Copyright Act 1962]

6.10C. In secondary entries, laws are entered as name-title headings.

> **United States.** Laws, etc.

> **New Zealand.** Copyright Act 1962

---

5. The rules given here cover only the most straightforward collections of laws. When dealing with more complex cases, including session laws of states (of the United States), codified laws, component parts, and collections other than those of states, consult *Library of Congress Rule Interpretations*.

6.11. TREATIES, ETC.

6.11A. Collections of treaties, etc. Use, as the uniform title for a collection of treaties and/or other agreements between two parties, *Treaties, etc.* followed by the name of the other party.

[25.16A1]

> **France**
> [Treaties, etc. Great Britain]

Use *Treaties, etc.* alone for a collection of treaties between one party and two or more other parties.

> **United States**
> [Treaties, etc.]

If a collection of treaties, etc., is identified by a collective name, use that name followed in parentheses by the year, earlier year, or earliest year of signing for an item containing all the treaties, etc. For a single treaty, etc., in the collection, see 6.11B. Make *see also* references from the title of the collection to the headings and/or titles of the single treaties.

> **Treaty of Utrecht** *(1713)*
> *see also*
>
> **France**
> [Treaties, etc. Prussia...]
>
> **Spain**
> [Treaties, etc. Great Britain...]
> [*etc.*]

6.11B. One treaty, etc.

6.11B1. Two or three parties. Use a uniform title beginning *Treaties, etc.* for a treaty or other agreement between two or three of the following:

- a) national governments
- b) international intergovernmental bodies
- c) the Holy See
- d) jurisdictions now below the national level but retaining treaty-making powers.

If there is only one party on the other side, add the name of the other party. Add the date, earlier date, or earliest date of signing in the form: year, abbreviated name of the month, number of the day.

[25.16B1]

> **Denmark**
> [Treaties, etc. Great Britain, 1966 Mar. 3]
> Agreement between the government of the United Kingdom of Great Britain and Northern Ireland and the kingdom of Denmark relating to the delimitation of the continental shelf between the two countries, London, 3 March 1966

Netherlands
[Treaties, etc. 1943 Oct. 21]
Convention monétaire belgo-luxembourgeoise-néerlandaise ... 21
oct. 1943
(*A treaty between the Netherlands on the one side and Belgium and Luxembourg on the other*)

6.11B2. Four or more parties. Use as the uniform title for a treaty, etc., between four or more parties the name by which the treaty is known. Use an English name if there is one. Add, in parentheses, the year, earlier year, or earliest year of signing. When making added entries for individual signatories to such an agreement, formulate the uniform title as instructed in 6.11B1.

[25.16B2]

Convention Regarding the Status of Aliens (*1928*)
Convención sobre condiciones de los extranjeros : celebrada entre los Estados Unidos Mexicanos y varias naciones : firmada en la ciudad de La Habana el 20 febrero de 1928

Treaty of Paris (*1763*)

Universal Copyright Convention (*1952*)

6.11B3. In forming secondary headings for treaties, etc., covered under 6.11A-6.11B1, use *Treaties, etc.* under the heading for the name of the government under which the treaty is entered.

France. Treaties, etc. Great Britain

Netherlands. Treaties, etc. 1943 Oct. 21

In forming secondary headings for treaties, etc., covered under 6.11B2 above, use the uniform title alone.

Treaty of Paris (*1763*)

Universal Copyright Convention (*1952*)

APPENDIX I

Examples of Catalog Records

This appendix contains examples of full cataloging records created using the rules in this manual. On facing pages are USMARC-tagged versions of the same records. These examples are based on real descriptions of real records, although in some cases the original descriptions may have been edited for use in this manual. The records described are held by Yale University (J.H. Lefroy journals, Queen Caroline collection, Henry Knox letters, Romain Truchard du Molin papers, and Kenneth McLeod Bissell diaries); Library of Congress (Russian-American Company records microfilm, J. Pierpont Morgan collection, and Bollingen Foundation records); U.S. National Archives (Bureau of Insular Affairs records); Alabama Department of Archives and History (Board of Social Work Examiners license files); New York Public Library (Vito Marcantonio collection); University of Oklahoma (American Indian Institute motion pictures); Harvard University (Lee Simonson designs and photographs); Charles Babbage Institute (History of Programming Languages Conference records); and Minnesota Historical Society (State Board of Corrections and Charities lantern slides).

Lefroy, J. H. (John Henry), Sir, 1817-1890.
    Journals, 1843 May 1-1844 Nov. 18.
    2 v. : ill.
    British army officer, surveyor, governor of Bermuda and Tasmania, and geographer.
    Includes scientific readings and notes for a magnetic surveying expedition to the
Northwest Territories of Canada; also contains financial accounts for the expedition and
comments, descriptions, and drawings relating to Indian tribes, geology, flora, and fauna
of the areas surveyed.
    Gift of Millicent Todd Bingham, ca. 1970.

Bollingen Foundation.
    Records, 1939-1973 (bulk 1965-1968).
    78,000 items.
    Philanthropy founded by Paul and Mary Conover Mellon to fund scholarly research
and publication in the general area of the humanities.
    Relates to the foundation's history and to its fellowship and contribution programs and
consists of correspondence, grant applications and reports, legal papers, minutes, clippings, and printed material, chiefly 1965-1968. Included are files relating to the awarding
of the Bollingen Prize in Poetry, the publication of the Bollingen Series by Princeton
University Press, and the publication of the collected works of Carl Jung and Paul Valéry.
Correspondents include John D. Barrett, Huntington Cairns, Malcolm Cowley, T.S. Eliot,
Abraham Flexner, Raymond B. Fosdick, Donald Gallup, Vaun Gillmor, Gotthard
Gunther, Irving Howe, Carl Jung, Erich Kahler, Sigfried Kracauer, Joseph W. Krutch,
Jacques Maritain, Paul Mellon, Erich Neumann, Maud Oakes, Paul Radin, Herbert Read,
Mary Ritter, Allen Tate, Mark Van Doren, Stanley Young, and Heinrich Zimmer.
    Gift of the Bollingen Foundation trustees, 1973.
    Access restricted.
    Finding aid in the library.

Caroline Amelia Elizabeth, Queen, consort of George IV, King of Great Britain,
    1768-1821.
    Collection of papers relating to Queen Caroline, 1797-1821.
    20 items.
    Papers focus on the controversy surrounding Queen Caroline, including 11 ALS from
Caroline to Thomas Wilde, and 8 ALS from various other figures involved, including
George Canning, the Earl of Eldon, Samuel Parr, and Edward Thurlow.
    Source unknown.

100	1-	$a	Lefroy, J. H. $q (John Henry), $c Sir, $d 1817-1890.
245	00	$k	Journals, $f 1843 May 1-1844 Nov. 18.
300	--	$a	2 $f v. : $b ill.
545	--	$a	British army officer, surveyor, governor of Bermuda and Tasmania, and geographer.
520	8-	$a	Includes scientific readings and notes for a magnetic surveying expedition to the Northwest Territories of Canada; also contains financial accounts for the expedition and comments, descriptions, and drawings relating to Indian tribes, geology, flora, and fauna of the areas surveyed.
541	--	$a	Gift of Millicent Todd Bingham, $d ca. 1970.

110	2-	$a	Bollingen Foundation.
245	00	$k	Records, $f 1939-1973 $g (bulk 1965-1968)
300	--	$a	78,000 $f items.
545	--	$a	Philanthropy founded by Paul and Mary Conover Mellon to fund scholarly research and publication in the general area of the humanities.
520	8-	$a	Relates to the foundation's history and to its fellowship and contribution programs and consists of correspondence, grant applications and reports, legal papers, minutes, clippings, and printed material, chiefly 1965-1968. $b Included are files relating to the awarding of the Bollingen Prize in Poetry, the publication of the Bollingen Series by Princeton University Press, and the publication of the collected works of Carl Jung and Paul Valéry. Correspondents include John D. Barrett, Huntington Cairns, Malcolm Cowley, T.S. Eliot, Abraham Flexner, Raymond B. Fosdick, Donald Gallup, Vaun Gillmor, Gotthard Gunther, Irving Howe, Carl Jung, Erich Kahler, Sigfried Kracauer, Joseph W. Krutch, Jacques Maritain, Paul Mellon, Erich Neumann, Maud Oakes, Paul Radin, Herbert Read, Mary Ritter, Allen Tate, Mark Van Doren, Stanley Young, and Heinrich Zimmer.
541	--	$a	Gift of the Bollingen Foundation trustees, $d 1973.
506	--	$a	Access restricted.
555	8-	$a	Finding aid in the library.

100	0-	$a	Caroline Amelia Elizabeth, $c Queen, consort of George IV, King of Great Britain, $d 1768-1821.
245	00	$a	Collection of papers relating to Queen Caroline, $f 1797-1821.
300	--	$a	20 $f items.
520	8-	$a	Papers focus on the controversy surrounding Queen Caroline, including 11 ALS from Caroline to Thomas Wilde, and 8 ALS from various other figures involved, including George Canning, the Earl of Eldon, Samuel Parr, and Edward Thurlow.
541	--	$a	Source unknown.

Rossiĭsko-amerikanskaĭa Kompaniĭa.

    Russian-American Company records, 1802-1867.

    104 microfilm reels.

    Created in 1799 by Czar Paul I as a monopoly to carry on the Russian fur trade on the North American continent, the Russian-American Company had political and economic control of Alaska until its purchase by the U.S. in 1867.

    Includes letters sent by the governors general (1818-1867, 40 v.); letters received by the governors general (1802, 1817-1866, 25 v.); and logs of vessels and journals of exploring expeditions (1842-1867, 20 v.).

    Microfilm.

    Originals in: National Archives and Records Administration (formerly at Sitka, Alaska, and the U.S. Department of State).

    In Russian longhand.

    Described in: University of California Bancroft Library: A Guide to the Manuscript Collections. Berkeley, Calif.: University of California, 1963.

Bissell, Kenneth McLeod, 1884-1972.

    Four years at Yale : diaries, 1903 Sept. 16-1907 Oct. 5.

    4 v.

    Student, Yale University class of 1907.

    Detailed account of the academic, social, cultural, and athletic life at Yale University; also contains accounts of summer vacations and a trip to Europe in the summer of 1906 and statistical data on the class of 1907.

    Gift of Mr. Bissell, 1956.

    Title transcribed from spine.

Knox, Henry, 1750-1806.

    Letters : Charleston, [S.C.], to Paul Hyacinte Perrault, 1794 July 9, 1794 Dec. 31.

    2 items.

    Relates to staff and expenses for the job of fortification of the port and harbor of Charleston, S.C.

Truchard du Molin, Romain, 1794?-1877.

    Papers, 1858-1877.

    1 v. (ca. 200 items).

    French jurist and magistrate.

    Correspondence between Romain Truchard du Molin and his friend and fellow magistrate, Augustine Chassaing, relating primarily to historical research Molin was pursuing on the baronies of Velay. Includes printed biographical notices of M. Truchard du Molin.

110	2-	$a	Rossiĭsko-amerikanskaiā Kompaniiā.
245	00	$a	Russian-American Company records, $f 1802-1867.
300	--	$a	104 $f microfilm reels.
545	--	$a	Created in 1799 by Czar Paul I as a monopoly to carry on the Russian fur trade on the North American continent, the Russian-American Company had political and economic control of Alaska until its purchase by the U.S. in 1867.
520	8-	$a	Includes letters sent by the governors general (1818-1867, 40 v.); letters received by the governors general (1802, 1817-1866, 25 v.); and logs of vessels and journals of exploring expeditions (1842-1867, 20 v.).
533	--	$a	Microfilm.
535	1-	$a	Originals in: National Archives and Records Administration (formerly at Sitka, Alaska, and the U.S. Department of State).
546	--	$a	In Russian longhand.
510	3-	$a	Described in: University of California Bancroft Library: A Guide to the Manuscript Collections. Berkeley, Calif.: University of California, 1963

100	1-	$a	Bissell, Kenneth McLeod, $d 1884-1972.
245	00	$a	Four years at Yale : $k diaries, $f 1903 Sept. 16-1907 Oct. 5.
300	--	$a	4 $f v.
545	--	$a	Student, Yale University class of 1907.
520	8-	$a	Detailed account of the academic, social, cultural, and athletic life at Yale University; also contains accounts of summer vacations and a trip to Europe in the summer of 1906 and statistical data on the class of 1907.
541	--	$a	Gift of Mr. Bissell, $d 1956.
500	--	$a	Title transcribed from spine.

100	1-	$a	Knox, Henry, $d 1750-1806.
245	00	$a	Letters : $b Charleston, [S.C.], to Paul Hyacinte Perrault, $f 1794 July 9, 1794 Dec. 31.
300	--	$a	2 $f items.
520	8-	$a	Relates to staff and expenses for the job of fortification of the port and harbor of Charleston, S.C.

100	2-	$a	Truchard du Molin, Romain, $d 1794?-1877.
245	00	$a	Papers, $f 1858-1877.
300	--	$a	1 $f v. (ca. 200 items).
545	--	$a	French jurist and magistrate.
520	8-	$a	Correspondence between Romain Truchard du Molin and his friend and fellow magistrate, Augustine Chassaing, relating primarily to historical research Molin was pursuing on the baronies of Velay. Includes printed biographical notices of M. Truchard du Molin.

Morgan, J. Pierpont (John Pierpont), 1837-1913, *collector.*
The John Pierpont Morgan collection of the signers of the Declaration of Independence, 1761-1803.
150 items.
Financier and collector.
Correspondence, documents, and portraits of the 56 signers of the Declaration of Independence; correspondence and portraits of Charles Thomson, secretary of the Continental Congress, and of John Nixon who first read the declaration to the public; facsimiles of the signers' signatures; original letter (1912 Nov. 19) of donation from Morgan and reply from William Howard Taft.
Also on microfilm (1 reel).
Collection originally begun by David McNeely Stauffer and completed by Mr. Morgan.
Gift of J.P. Morgan, 1912.

United States. Bureau of Insular Affairs.
Records, 1868-1945.
1,645 cubic ft.
Founded 13 Dec. 1898, as the Division of Customs and Insular Affairs in the Office of the Secretary of War to assist in administering customs and other civil affairs in Puerto Rico, Cuba, and the Philippine Islands; designated Division of Insular Affairs, 10 Dec. 1900, and Bureau of Insular Affairs by an act of 1 July 1902; Reorganization Plan No. II of 1939 consolidated the bureau with the Division of Territories and Island Possessions, Department of the Interior.
Record Group 350 includes general records (1898-1945, 922 ft.); other records relating to the Philippine Islands (1897-1938, 47 ft.); library records (1868-1945, 685 ft.); miscellaneous records (1898-1937, 49 ft.); and audiovisual records (1898-1939, 14,750 items).
Forms part of: Records of the Department of the Interior.
Described in: Guide to the National Archives of the United States. Washington, D.C.: National Archives, 1974.

Alabama. Board of Social Work Examiners.
Expired/inactive license computer files, 1977- .
1 computer disk.
Arrangement: Alphabetical.
Computer (floppy disk) files of persons with expired/inactive social worker licenses. Each applicant's file records the name, last known address, license number, level of license, how licensed, and year initially licensed. An annual printout is generated.
Unrestricted.

100	1-	$a	Morgan, J. Pierpont $q (John Pierpont), $d 1837-1913, $e collector.
245	00	$a	The John Pierpont Morgan collection of the signers of the Declaration of Independence, $f 1761-1803.
300	--	$a	150 $f items.
545	--	$a	Financier and collector.
520	8-	$a	Correspondence, documents, and portraits of the 56 signers of the Declaration of Independence; correspondence and portraits of Charles Thomson, secretary of the Continental Congress, and of John Nixon, who first read the declaration to the public; facsimiles of the signers' signatures; original letter (1912 Nov. 19) of donation from Morgan and reply from William Howard Taft.
530	--	$a	Also on microfilm (1 reel).
561	--	$a	Collection originally begun by David McNeely Stauffer and completed by Mr. Morgan.
541	--	$a	Gift of J.P. Morgan, $d 1912.

110	1-	$a	United States. $b Bureau of Insular Affairs.
245	00	$a	Records, $f 1868-1945.
300	--	$a	1,645 $f cubic ft.
545	--	$a	Founded 13 Dec. 1898, as the Division of Customs and Insular Affairs in the Office of the Secretary of War to assist in administering customs and other civil affairs in Puerto Rico, Cuba, and the Philippine Islands; designated Division of Insular Affairs, 10 Dec. 1900, and Bureau of Insular Affairs by an act of 1 July 1902; Reorganization Plan No. II of 1939 consolidated the bureau with the Division of Territories and Island Possessions, Department of the Interior.
520	8-	$a	Record Group 350 includes general records (1898-1945, 922 ft.); other records relating to the Philippine Islands (1897-1938, 47 ft.); library records (1868-1945, 685 ft.); miscellaneous records (1898-1937, 49 ft.); and audiovisual records, (1898-1939, 14,750 items).
580	--	$a	Forms part of: Records of the Department of the Interior.
510	3-	$a	Described in: Guide to the National Archives of the United States. Washington, D.C.: National Archives, 1974

110	1-	$a	Alabama. $b Board of Social Work Examiners.
245	00	$a	Expired/inactive license computer files, $f 1977-[ongoing].
300	--	$a	1 $f computer disk.
351	--	$a	Arrangement: Alphabetical.
520	8-	$a	Computer (floppy disk) files of persons with expired/inactive social worker licenses. Each applicant's file records the name, last known address, license number, level of license, how licensed, and year initially licensed. An annual printout is generated.
506	--	$a	Unrestricted.

Marcantonio, Vito, 1902-1954.

Collection of political speeches and advertisements, 1938-1952.

6 sound tapes.

Vito Marcantonio was a New York politician active from the early 1930s up to his death in 1954. He was a congressman for the 18th New York District from 1935 to 1937 and from 1939 to 1951. He ran unsuccessfully for mayor of New York City in 1949. He was a member of the American Labor Party.

The collection of sound recordings dates from 1938 to 1952. Several selections consist of political advertisements for the 1949 mayoral campaign. Others include a 1951 press conference with an assistant to Marcantonio, Clifford T. McAvoy, who was running for City Council; a political speech given by Marcantonio in 1938 to the Harlem Legislative Committee; a 1943 speech on the downfall of Mussolini; and a 1952 speech given to the American Labor Party.

Contents for individual reels on containers.

Tape reels transferred from original acetate discs.

American Indian Institute.

Motion pictures, ca. 1940-1970.

19 items.

Black-and-white and color 16 mm. films, commercially produced for educational purposes, depicting sign language, a pipe ceremony, a war dance, a Navajo and a Sioux family, a Hopi settlement, an Indian fashion show, a Creek stickball game, and the Concho (Oklahoma) Indian School.

American Indian Institute Manuscript Collection also in repository.

Gift of Boyce Timmons.

Inventory available in repository.

Simonson, Lee, 1888-1967.

Designs and photographs of Lee Simonson, 1919-1938.

ca. 100 items.

American theatrical designer. Simonson was one of the founders and directors of the Theatre Guild, and director of the American National Theatre and Academy, the Museum of Costume Art (New York), and the International Exhibition of Theatre Art (New York, 1934).

Contains costume and scenery designs, technical drawings, blueprints, and photographs of settings by Simonson.

Gift of Lee Simonson, 1964.

Manuscript catalog available in repository.

Cite as: Lee Simonson Papers. Harvard Theatre Collection.

100   **1-**   **$a**   Marcantonio, Vito, **$d** 1902-1954.

245   **00**   **$a**   Collection of political speeches and advertisements, **$f** 1938-1952.

300   **--**   **$a**   6 sound tapes.

545   **--**   **$a**   Vito Marcantonio was a New York politician active from the early 1930s up to his death in 1954. He was a congressman for the 18th New York District from 1935 to 1937 and from 1939 to 1951. He ran unsuccessfully for mayor of New York City in 1949. He was a member of the American Labor Party.

520   **8-**   **$a**   The collection of sound recordings dates from 1938 to 1952. Several selections consist of political advertisements for the 1949 mayoral campaign. Others include a 1951 press conference with an assistant to Marcantonio, Clifford T. McAvoy, who was running for City Council; a political speech given by Marcantonio in 1938 to the Harlem Legislative Committee; a 1943 speech on the downfall of Mussolini; and a 1952 speech given to the American Labor Party.

555   **0-**   **$a**   Contents for individual reels on containers.

500   **--**   **$a**   Tape reels transferred from original acetate discs.

110   **2-**   **$a**   American Indian Institute.

245   **00**   **$k**   Motion pictures, **$f** ca. 1940-1970.

300   **--**   **$a**   19 items.

520   **8-**   **$a**   Black-and-white and color 16 mm. films, commercially produced for educational purposes, depicting sign language, a pipe ceremony, a war dance, a Navajo and a Sioux family, a Hopi settlement, an Indian fashion show, a Creek stickball game, and the Concho (Oklahoma) Indian School.

500   **--**   **$a**   American Indian Institute Manuscript Collection also in repository.

541   **--**   **$a**   Gift of Boyce Timmons.

555   **0-**   **$a**   Inventory available in repository.

100   **1-**   **$a**   Simonson, Lee, **$d** 1888-

245   **00**   **$a**   Designs and photographs of Lee Simonson, **$f** 1919-1938.

300   **--**   **$a**   ca. 100 items.

545   **--**   **$a**   American theatrical designer. Simonson was one of the founders and directors of the Theatre Guild, and director of the American National Theatre and Academy, the Museum of Costume Art (New York), and the International Exhibition of Theatre Art (New York, 1934).

520   **8-**   **$a**   Contains costume and scenery designs, technical drawings, blueprints, and photographs of settings by Simonson.

541   **--**   **$a**   Gift of Lee Simonson, **$d** 1964.

555   **0-**   **$a**   Manuscript catalog available in repository.

524   **--**   **$a**   Lee Simonson Papers. Harvard Theatre Collection.

History of Programming Languages Conference (1978 : Los Angeles, Calif.)
Records, 1959, 1972-1983 (bulk 1976-1982).
7 cubic ft.

The History of Programming Languages Conference was organized by the Special Interest Group in Programming Languages of the Association for Computing Machinery, and took place in Los Angeles on 1-3 June 1978. The purpose of the conference was to provide a written record for programming languages that were created by 1967, remained in use by 1977, and influenced the field of computing. Speakers included those who had played a major part in the development and use of ALGOL, APL, APT, BASIC, COBOL, FORTRAN, GPSS, JOSS, JOVIAL, LISP, PL/I, SIMULA, and SNOBOL. Jean E. Sammet served as general and program committee chairman, and John A.N. Lee was the administrative chairman. Proceedings of the conference were edited by Richard L. Wexelblat and published in 1981.

Correspondence, reports, draft presentations, newspaper clippings, notes, memoranda, National Science Foundation grant records, publicity materials, and mailing lists relating to the planning and organization of the conference. Also includes conference proceedings in the form of black-and-white video cassettes, reel-to-reel and cassette audio recordings, black-and-white photographs, slides, transcripts of presentations, preprints of papers, and book drafts. Correspondents include Herbert R.J. Grosch, John A.N. Lee, Jean E. Sammet, and Richard L. Wexelblat.

Researchers require permission from the Charles Babbage Institute for access to the collection until 1 January 2004.

Copyright of portions of the collection owned by the Association for Computing Machinery.

Unpublished folder list available from repository.

Proceedings published in: Wexelblat, Richard L., ed. History of Programming Languages. New York: Academic Press, 1981.

Minnesota. State Board of Corrections and Charities.
Lantern slides of poorhouses, [190-].
Lantern slides: 15 items.
Reference prints: 15 items.

Images of poorhouses in the following Minnesota counties: Otter Tail, Pipestone, Ramsey, Rice, Rock, Wabasha, Washington, and Winona.

Found, along with correspondence of the Minnesota State Board of Corrections and Charities, in a vault formerly occupied by the Motor Vehicle Division, Room 27, State Capitol. Otherwise undocumented.

Transferred to Archives, 31 August 1955.

111	**2-**	**$a**	History of Programming Languages Conference **$d** (1978 : **$c** Los Angeles, Calif.)
245	**00**	**$k**	Records, **$f** 1959, 1972-1983 **$g** (bulk 1976-1982).
300	**--**	**$a**	7 **$f** cubic ft.
545	**--**	**$a**	The History of Programming Languages Conference was organized by the Special Interest Group in Programming Languages of the Association for Computing Machinery, and took place in Los Angeles on 1-3 June 1978. The purpose of the conference was to provide a written record for programming languages that were created by 1967, remained in use by 1977, and influenced the field of computing. Speakers included those who had played a major part in the development and use of ALGOL, APL, APT, BASIC, COBOL, FORTRAN, GPSS, JOSS, JOVIAL, LISP, PL/I, SIMULA, and SNOBOL. Jean E. Sammet served as general and program committee chairman, and John A.N. Lee was the administrative chairman. Proceedings of the conference were edited by Richard L. Wexelblat and published in 1981.
520	**8-**	**$a**	Correspondence, reports, draft presentations, newspaper clippings, notes, memoranda, National Science Foundation grant records, publicity materials, and mailing lists relating to the planning and organization of the conference. Also includes conference proceedings in the form of black-and-white video cassettes, reel-to-reel and cassette audio recordings, black-and-white photographs, slides, transcripts of presentations, preprints of papers, and book drafts. Correspondents include Herbert R.J. Grosch, John A.N. Lee, Jean E. Sammet, and Richard L. Wexelblat.
506	**--**	**$a**	Researchers require permission from the Charles Babbage Institute for access to the collection until 1 January 2004.
540	**--**	**$a**	Copyright of portions of the collection owned by the Association for Computing Machinery.
555	**0-**	**$a**	Unpublished folder list available from repository.
581	**8-**	**$a**	Proceedings published in: Wexelblat, Richard L., ed. History Of Programming Languages. New York: Academic Press, 1981.

110	**1-**	**$a**	Minnesota. **$b** State Board of Corrections and Charities.
245	**00**	**$a**	Lantern slides of poorhouses, [190-].
300	**--**	**$3**	Lantern slides: **$a** 15 items.
300	**--**	**$3**	Reference prints: **$a** 15 items.
520	**8-**	**$a**	Images of poorhouses in the following Minnesota counties: Otter Tail, Pipestone, Ramsey, Rice, Rock, Wabasha, Washington, and Winona.
561	**--**	**$a**	Found, along with correspondence of the Minnesota State Board of Corrections and Charities, in a vault formerly occupied by the Motor Vehicle Division, Room 27, State Capitol. Otherwise undocumented.
541	**--**	**$a**	Transferred to Archives, **$d** 31 August 1955.

APPENDIX II

USMARC-AMC Tagging of Examples

This appendix contains USMARC-tagged versions of most of the examples given in the cataloging rules in this manual. The examples are arranged by rule number so that users can easily move back and forth between the rule and the coded version of the examples.

These examples are intended to help readers understand the relationship between the USMARC format, AACR 2, and APPM. They cannot be considered authoritative for all circumstances. In preparing cataloging for encoding into a USMARC-based system, the input manuals and conventions for that system *must* be consulted. The Library of Congress Name Authority File should be consulted for the authorized forms of personal and corporate name headings.

All examples of personal and corporate name headings and uniform title headings are given as main entry headings (i.e., 1XX), except where the rule specifically relates to their use in secondary entries. It should be understood that the same tagging generally also applies when the headings are used as subject added entries (6XX) or as added entries (7XX). The only significant difference will be in the value of the second indicator.

In cases where indicators must be assigned based on the needs of a particular catalog, the indicators have been chosen arbitrarily (e.g., the first indicator in field 245 has always been set to *0*, for "no title added entry"). When an indicator is blank, this is represented by a hyphen.

Although the actual MARC subfield delimiter is a double dagger, the subfield delimiter is often conventionally represented by a dollar sign ($), which is used in these examples. In addition, the spacing between content designators and data elements as given here is dictated by the need for typographical clarity; individual systems may have different requirements.

CHAPTER 1 DESCRIPTION OF ARCHIVAL MATERIAL

1.1B1

    245 00 $a Sophie's choice, **$f** 1979.

    245 00 $a Christian ethics and precepts, **$f** 1846-1852.

1.1B4

    245 00 $k Records, **$f** 1917-1967.

    245 00 $k Papers, **$f** 1888-1920.

    245 00 $k Collection, **$f** 1787-1826.

1.1B5

    245 00 $a Special charge vouchers, **$f** 1940-[ongoing]

    245 00 $k Papers, **$f** 1703-1908 **$g** (bulk 1780-1835)

    100 1- $a Hamilton, Alexander, **$d** 1757-1804.

    245 00 $k Papers, **$f** 1703-1908 **$g** (bulk 1780-1835)

| 100 | 1- | $a | Hamilton, Alexander, $d 1757-1804. |
| 245 | 00 | $a | Alexander Hamilton papers, $f 1703-1908 $g (bulk 1780-1835) |

| 100 | 1- | $a | Flanner, Janet, $d 1892- |
| 245 | 00 | $a | Janet Flanner-Solita Solano papers, $f 1870-1975. |

| 100 | 1- | $a | Dumont, Henry, $d 1878-1949. |
| 245 | 00 | $a | Henry and Nina Webster Dumont papers, $f 1905-1936. |

| 100 | 3- | $a | Schramm family. |
| 245 | 00 | $k | Papers, $f 1932-1971. |

| 100 | 1- | $a | Richardson, James Burchell. |
| 245 | 00 | $a | Family papers, $f 1803-1910. |

| 245 | 00 | $a | Short-Harrison-Symmes family papers, $f 1760-1878. |

| 110 | 2- | $a | Bollingen Foundation. |
| 245 | 00 | $k | Records, $f 1939-1973. |

| 110 | 2- | $a | Bollingen Foundation. |
| 245 | 00 | $a | Bollingen Foundation records, $f 1939-1973. |

or

| 245 | 00 | $a | Records of the Bollingen Foundation, $f 1939-1973. |

| 110 | 1- | $a | United States. $b Office of the Comptroller of the Currency. $b Examining Division. |
| 245 | 00 | $k | Records, $f 1863-1935. |

| 110 | 2- | $a | Northwestern University (Evanston, Ill). $b Office of Student Aid. |
| 245 | 00 | $a | Financial aid files, $f 1955-1965. |

| 110 | 1- | $a | New York (State). $b Supreme Court of Judicature (Albany). |
| 245 | 00 | $a | Assignments of error, $f 1837-1847 $g (bulk 1837-1839, 1844-1847) |

| 110 | 1- | $a | Minnesota. $b State Board of Corrections and Charities. |
| 245 | 00 | $a | Lantern slides of poorhouses, $f [190-] |

| 110 | 1- | $a | Alabama. $b Board of Social Work Examiners. |
| 245 | 00 | $a | Expired/inactive license computer files, $f 1977-[ongoing] |

| 100 | 1- | $a | Porter, John K. $q (John Kilham), $d 1819-1892, $e collector. |
| 245 | 00 | $a | Autograph collection, $f 1600-1882. |

| 100 | 1- | $a | Porter, John K. $q (John Kilham), $d 1819-1892, $e collector. |
| 245 | 00 | $a | John K. Porter autograph collection, $f 1600-1882. |

| 100 | 1- | $a | Purland, Theodosius, $e collector. |
| 245 | 00 | $a | Collection of papers on mesmerism, $f 1842-1854. |

| 245 | 00 | $a | Harkness collection, $f 1525-1651. |

154

245 **00** **$a** Shaker collection, **$f** 1792-1937.

245 **00** **$a** Portuguese manuscripts collection, **$f** 1345-1918.

245 **00** **$a** California travel diaries, **$f** 1849-1851.

245 **00** **$k** Correspondence, **$f** 1804-1828.

245 **00** **$k** Diaries, **$f** [1897?]-1915.

245 **00** **$k** Logbook, **$f** 1818-[ca.1823].

245 **00** **$a** Ebenezer Sprout-William Shepard orderly book, **$f** 1779-1780.

245 **00** **$k** Diary, **$f** 1789 Jan. 1-1791 Mar. 17.

100 **1-** **$a** Sutherland, Alan D., **$d** 1897- , **$e** interviewee.
245 **00** **$a** Typewritten transcript of oral history interview : **$b** Brattleboro, Vt., with John Duffy and Martin Kaufman, **$f** 1968 June 15.

1.1D1

245 **00** **$a** Twenty love poems and a song of despair = **$b** 20 poemas de amor y una canción desesperada, **$f** 1976.

1.1E1

245 **00** **$k** Lecture : **$b** Royal College of Medicine, London, **$f** [18--]
245 **00** **$k** Letter : **$b** Dublin, to Henrik Ibsen, Kristiania [Oslo], **$f** 1901 Mar 6.
245 **00** **$k** ALS : **$b** Worcester Park, Surrey, to George Gissing, Rome, **$f** [ca. 1891 Jan 1].
245 **00** **$k** Holograph petition : **$b** to James Monroe, **$f** 1813 July 1.
245 **00** **$a** Sophie's choice : **$k** holograph, **$f** 1979.
245 **00** **$a** Diamond Lil : **$k** playscript, **$f** 1928.
245 **00** **$a** Christian ethics and precepts : **$k** commonplace book, **$f** 1846-1852.
245 **04** **$a** The need of redirected rural schools : **$b** address before the Iowa State Teachers Association, Des Moines : **$k** type-script, **$f** 1910 Oct. 4.

1.1F

245 **04** **$a** The charity ball : **$b** a comedy in four acts : **$k** typescript, **$f** 1889 / **$c** by David Belasco and Henry C. DeMille.
245 **00** **$a** Divorce : **$k** holograph, **$f** [187-?] / **$c** by Augustin Daly.

1.2B1

250 **--** **$a** Prelim. draft.
250 **--** **$a** 1st script.
[*etc.*]

1.2C1

250 **--** **$a** Continuity / **$b** written by Waldemar Young.
[*etc.*]

1.5B1

    300 -- **$a** 87 **$f** items **$a** (0.5 **$f** linear ft.)
or
    300 -- **$a** 87 **$f** items (0.5 linear ft.)
or
    300 -- **$a** 87 items (0.5 linear ft.)
[*etc.*]

    300 -- **$a** ca. 10,200 **$f** items **$a** (14.7 **$f**linear ft.)
    300 -- **$a** 14.7 **$f** linear ft. **$a** (ca. 10,200 **$f** items)
    300 -- **$a** 128 **$f** linear ft.
    300 -- **$a** 40 **$f** cubic meters.
    300 -- **$a** 6 **$f** v. **$a** (1.5 **$f** linear ft.)
    300 -- **$a** 12 **$f** linear ft. **$a** (36 **$f** boxes)

    300 -- **$a** 1500 **$f** items.
    300 -- **$a** 2 **$f** microfilm reels.
                  [*field 300 is repeatable for multiple statements of extent*]

    300 -- **$3** Diaries: **$a** 17 **$f** v.
    300 -- **$3** Correspondence: **$a** 0.5 linear **$f** ft.
    300 -- **$3** Architectural drawings: **$a** 6 **$f** items.

1.5B2

    300 -- **$a** 1 **$f** item (47 p.)
    300 -- **$a** 1 **$f** v. (32 leaves)
    300 -- **$a** 1 **$f** v. (ca. 500 items)

1.5B3

    300 -- **$a** 450 **$f** items.
    300 -- **$a** 2 **$f** microfilm reels.
optionally
    300 -- **$3** Originals: **$a** 450 **$f** items.
    300 -- **$3** Copies: **$a** 2 **$f** microfilm reels.

    300 -- **$a** 123 **$f** microfilm reels.
    300 -- **$a** 4 **$f** microfiches.
    300 -- **$a** 1 **$f** microopaque.
    300 -- **$a** 3 **$f** ft. of microfilm.
    300 -- **$a** 1 **$f** microfilm reel (12 ft.)
    300 -- **$a** 1 **$f** microfiche (120 frames)
    300 -- **$a** Partial microfilm reel.

1.5C1

    300 -- **$a** 1 **$f** microfilm reel (220 frames) : **$b** negative.
    300 -- **$a** 147 **$f** microfilm reels : **$b** negative.
    300 -- **$a** 20 **$f** leaves : **$b** vellum.
    300 -- **$a** 6 **$f** v. : **$b** ill.
    300 -- **$a** 1 **$f** v. : **$b** bound in vellum.

1.5D1

    300 -- **$a** 6 **$f** v. ; **$c** 30 cm.
    300 -- **$a** 20 **$f** items ; **$c** 20 x 30 cm.

300 -- **$a** 10 **$f** v. ; **$c** 28 cm. or smaller.

300 -- **$a** 12 **$f** linear ft. **$a** (28 **$f** boxes) ; **$g** 26 x 13 x 39 cm.

1.5D2

300 -- **$a** 1 **$f** item (6 p.) ; **$c** 24 cm.

300 -- **$a** 1 **$f** item (7 p.) ; **$c** 24 x 30 cm.

300 -- **$a** 1 **$f** item (12 leaves) ; **$c** 20 cm. folded to 10 x 12 cm.

300 -- **$a** 1 **$f** item (1 leaf) : **$b** parchment ; **$c** 35 x 66 cm. folded to 10 x 19 cm.

300 -- **$a** 1 **$f** v. (131 leaves in case) ; **$c** 26 cm.

300 -- **$a** 1 **$f** item (70 p. in case) ; **$c** 20 x 24 cm.

1.5D3

300 -- **$a** 20 **$f** aperture cards ; **$c** 9 x 19 cm.

300 -- **$a** 30 **$f** microfiches ; **$c** 10 x 15 cm.

300 -- **$a** 110 **$f** microfilm cassettes : **$b** negative ; **$c** 16 mm.

300 -- **$a** 1 **$f** microfilm reel (28 ft.) ; **$c** 16 mm.

1.7B

Note fields that contain detailed content designation can be rendered with that detail if the purpose is to sort on the various data elements that make up the subfields. If there is no intent to retrieve that data, however, the content designation can be largely ignored. To optimize retrieval on content designated subfields, introductory wording can be omitted. Examples will be given below showing both approaches. The examples of longer notes are not shown in their entirety, only to the extent necessary to make their content designation clear.

1.7B1

545 -- **$a** Nurse and leader of the birth control movement.

545 -- **$a** Established in the War Department, 3 Mar. 1865, to supervise all activities relating to refugees and freedmen and to assume custody...

545 -- **$a** Historian, of Wilson, Raleigh, and Chapel Hill, N.C.; first archivist of the United States; secretary of the North Carolina Historical Commission; professor at the University of North Carolina-Chapel Hill; and author.

1.7B2

520 8- **$a** Correspondence, essays, and notebooks covering the period when White was serving in the American embassy in Berlin....

520 8- **$a** Correspondence, diaries (1914-1953), articles, speeches, lectures, clippings, scrapbooks, printed matter, photographs, memorabilia, and organizational records relating to Mrs. Sanger's extensive activities on behalf of birth control in the U.S. and throughout the world. **$b** Includes material relating to many national and international congresses and conferences organized by Mrs. Sanger, her campaign to enlist public support for federal legislation on birth control,

157

and material relating to her interest and activity in Socialist politics and liberal reform groups....

520 **8-** **$a** Holograph petition of Burns to James Monroe, secretary of state, to obtain a letter of marque and reprisal for the schooner Snap Dragon, New Bern, N.C.

[*etc.*]

1.7B3

580 **--** **$a** Forms part of: Naval Historical Foundation manuscript collection.

580 **--** **$a** Forms part of: War Department collection of Confederate records (Record Group 109)

580 **--** **$a** In: Oppenheimer, J. Robert, 1904-1967. Papers, 1927-1967.
or
773 **0-** **$7** p1bc **$a** Oppenheimer, J. Robert, 1904-1967. **$t** Papers, 1927-1967.[1]

1.7B4

530 **--** **$a** Diaries and correspondence available on microfilm for use in repository only.

530 **--** **$a** Also available on microfilm; **$b** source: Library of Congress Photoduplication Service, Washington, D.C. 20540; **$d** order number: 18,447.

1.7B5

533 **--** **$3** In part, **$a** photocopies. **$b** Copied at: University of North Carolina at Chapel Hill, Southern Historical Collection; **$d** 1978.

533 **--** **$a** Photocopies (negative). **$b** Copied at: Archives Nationales, Paris, France; **$d** 1937.

533 **--** **$a** Microfilm; originals destroyed after filming.

533 **--** **$a** Microfilm. **$b** Duke University Library, Manuscript Department; **$c** University Publications of America **$d** 1987. **$e** 5 microfilm reels (nos. 18-22); **$f** (Records of antebellum plantations, series F, selections from the Manuscript Department, Duke University Library, part 1)

1.7B6

535 **1-** **$a** Originals in:[2] Manuscripts and Archives, Yale University Library; **$b** Box 1603A Yale Station, New Haven, Conn. 06520

535 **1-** **$3** Originals of diaries in: **$a** Manuscript Division, Library of Congress; **$b** Washington, D.C. 20540

---

1. Here, the introductory wording *In:* is presumed to be a display constant that is system generated.

2. In some systems, introductory wording may be automatically generated based on the value of the first indicator.

1.7B7

351	--	**$a**	Organized into the following series: I. General correspondence, 1812-1868; II. William Q. Force papers, 1843-1944...
351	--	**$b**	Arrangement: Chronological within record type (minutes, general memoranda, legislative memoranda, etc.) in each volume.
351	--	**$a**	Diaries and notebooks arranged chronologically, 1846-1903; family correspondence arranged chronologically, 1789-1825; ...

or

351	--	**$3**	Diaries and notebooks **$a** arranged chronologically, 1846-1903.
351	--	**$3**	Family correspondence **$a** arranged chronologically, 1789-1825.

[*etc.*]

1.7B8

546	--	**$a**	In Swedish.
546	--	**$a**	Chiefly in Russian longhand.

[*etc.*]

1.7B9

561	--	**$a**	Originally collected by George Madison and arranged by his nephew, John Ferris, after Madison's death. Purchased by Henry Kapper in 1878 who added to the collection with materials purchased at auctions in Philadelphia and Paris, 1878-1879.

[*etc.*]

1.7B10

541	--	**$c**	Gift; **$a** Worthington C. Ford; **$d** 1907.

[*or*]

541	--	**$a**	Ford, Worthington C.; **$c** gift; **$d** 1907.

[*or*]

541	--	**$a**	Gift of Worthington C. Ford, **$d** 1907.
541	--	**$a**	Source unknown.
541	--	**$c**	Purchase; **$d** 1978.
541	--	**$a**	Deposit, 1903. Converted to gift, 1948.

or

541	--	**$c**	Deposit, **$d** 1903.
541	--	**$c**	Converted to gift, **$d** 1948.
541	--	**$3**	Orderly books: **$c** Transfer; **$a** Pension Office; **$d** 1909.
541	--	**$3**	Letter books: **$c** Transfer; **$a** State Department; **$d** 1909.

1.7B11

506	--	**$a**	Access restricted.
506	--	**$a**	Closed to investigators until 1999.

506	--	**$a**	Classified under national security provisions; **$b** Department of Defense; **$e** Title 50, Chapter 401, U.S.C.

1.7B12

540	--	**$a**	Information on literary rights available in the repository.
540	--	**$a**	Copyright interests have been reserved.
540	--	**$a**	Photocopying of diaries is prohibited.

1.7B13

555	8-	**$a**	Finding aid in the repository; **$c** folder level control.
555	--	**$a**	Card index in the repository.
555	8-	**$a**	Described in: **$d** Library of Congress. Manuscript Division. Naval Historical Foundation Manuscript Collection: A Catalog. Washington, D.C.: Library of Congress, 1974.

1.7B14

510	3-	**$a**	Described in:[3] Library of Congress Acquisitions: Manuscript Division, 1979. Washington, D.C.: Library of Congress, 1981
510	4-	**$a**	Listed in: Ricci. Census, **$c** vol. 1, p. 857, no. 4
510	3-	**$3**	Arctic field notebooks cited in: **$a** Day, Harold. "Statistical Methods for Population Transport Estimation." Journal of Ecological Studies **$c** 7 (1974): 187

1.7B15

524	--	**$a**	James Hazen Hyde Papers, 1891-1941, New-York Historical Society[4]
524	--	**$a**	Socialist Party of America Records, Manuscript Department, Duke University Library

1.7B16

581	--	**$a**	Levine, Lawrence W. "William Shakespeare and the American People: A Study in Cultural Transformation." American Historical Review 89 (February 1984).[5]
581	--	**$a**	Poetry: A Magazine of Verse 59 (1942): 295-308.
581	8-	**$a**	Photographs published in: Mirer, Emma. Faces of Political Women. Boston: Whitehurst Press, 1984.

1.7B17

500	--	**$a**	Text heavily foxed.
500	--	**$a**	Title transcribed from spine.
500	--	**$a**	Also known as: Anglo-Dutch War collection.
500	--	**$a**	Tape reels transferred from original acetate discs.

---

3. In some systems, the introductory word *References:* may be displayed automatically based on the value of the first indicator.

4. In some systems, the introductory phrase *Cite as:* may be displayed automatically.

5. In some systems, the introductory word *Publications:* may be displayed automatically based on the "blank" as the value for the first indicator.

CHAPTER 2 CHOICE OF ACCESS POINTS

2.1A1

| 100 | 1- | $a | Hamilton, Alexander, $d 1757-1804. |
| 245 | 00 | $k | Papers, $f 1703-1908. |

| 100 | 1- | $a | Bissell, Kenneth McLeod, $d 1884-1972. |
| 245 | 00 | $a | Four years at Yale :$k diaries, $f 1903 Sept. 16-1907 Oct. 5. |

2.1A2

| 100 | 1- | $a | Flanner, Janet, 1892- |
| 245 | 00 | $a | Janet Flanner-Solita Solano papers, $f 1870-1975. |

| 100 | 1- | $a | Dumont, Henry, 1878-1949. |
| 245 | 00 | $a | Henry and Nina Webster Dumont papers, $f 1905-1936. |

2.1A3

| 100 | 3- | $a | Schramm family. |
| 245 | 00 | $k | Papers, $f 1932-1971. |

| 100 | 1- | $a | Richardson, James Burchell. |
| 245 | 00 | $k | Family papers, $f 1803-1910. |

2.1A4

| 100 | 1- | $a | Porter, John K. $q (John Kilham), $d 1819-1892, $e collector. |
| 245 | 00 | $a | John K. Porter autograph collection, $f 1600-1882. |

| 100 | 1- | $a | Purland, Theodosius, $e collector. |
| 245 | 00 | $a | Collection of papers on mesmerism, 1842-1854. |

| 100 | 1- | $a | Morgan, J. Pierpont $q (John Pierpont), $d 1837-1913, $e collector. |
| 245 | 04 | $a | The John Pierpont Morgan collection of the signers of the Declaration of Independence, $f 1761-1803. |

2.1A5

| 100 | 1- | $a | Styron, William, $d 1925- |
| 245 | 00 | $a | Sophie's choice : $k holograph / $c by William Styron. |

| 100 | 1- | $a | Burns, Otway, $d 1775-1850. |
| 245 | 00 | $k | Petition : $b to James Monroe, $f 1813 July 1. |

| 100 | 1- | $a | Washington, Bushrod, $d 1762-1829. |
| 245 | 00 | $k | ALS : $b to Henry Lee, $f 1810 Sept. 12. |

| 100 | 1- | $a | Morse, Samuel Finley Breese, $d 1791-1872. |
| 245 | 00 | $k | Letters : $b to Mrs. Silliman, $f 1845 Jan 1-Oct. 13. |

2.1A6

100	**1-**	**$a**	Wiesel, Elie, **$d** 1928- **$e** interviewee.
245	**00**	**$a**	Typed transcript of oral history interview, Duke University, Durham, N.C., **$f** 1987 Nov. 10.
110	**2-**	**$a**	Duke University. **$b** Living History Program.
245	**00**	**$a**	Oral history collection, **$f** 1968-1988.

2.1B2

110	**2-**	**$a**	Bollingen Foundation.
245	**00**	**$k**	Records, **$f** 1939-1973.
110	**2-**	**$a**	Auburn University. **$b** Division of Student Services.
245	**00**	**$a**	Dean of Student Service records, **$f** 1965-1980.
110	**1-**	**$a**	United States. **$b** Bureau of Insular Affairs.
245	**00**	**$k**	Records, **$f** 1868-1945.

2.1B3

110	**1-**	**$a**	New York (State). **$b** Dept. of Social Services.
245	**00**	**$a**	Reports of poorhouses, **$f** 1876-1940.
710	**11**	**$a**	New York (State). **$b** State Board of Charities. **$t** Reports of poorhouses, 1876-1910.
710	**11**	**$a**	New York (State). **$b** Dept. of Mental Hygiene. **$t** Reports of poorhouses, 1910-1920.

2.1B5

110	**1-**	**$a**	Wake County (N.C.)
245	**00**	**$k**	Land indenture, **$f** 1845 Oct. 15.
110	**1-**	**$a**	Burlington (Wis.). **$b** Mayor.
245	**00**	**$a**	May Day proclamation, **$f** 1959 May 1.

2.1C2

245	**00**	**$a**	Harkness collection, **$f** 1525-1651.
245	**00**	**$a**	Shaker collection, **$f** 1792-1937.

2.1C3

245	**00**	**$a**	Ebenezer Sprout-William Shepard orderly book, **$f** 1779-1780.

2.1C4

245	**00**	**$a**	Forest History Society oral history interviews, **$f** 1957-1960.

2.1C5

245	**00**	**$a**	Short-Harrison-Symmes family papers, **$f** 1760-1878.
700	**31**	**$a**	Short family.
700	**31**	**$a**	Harrison family.
700	**31**	**$a**	Symmes family.

2.1C6

245	**00**	**$a**	Analecta anglicana : **$k** commonplace books.
245	**00**	**$a**	New Bern Civil War collection.

2.3F

700	**12**	**$a**	Force, William Q. **$t** Papers, 1843-1944.
710	**12**	**$a**	College of St. Paul. **$t** Financial records, 1858 Jan 1-1861 Dec. 31.
710	**12**	**$a**	Margaret Sanger Research Bureau. **$t** Records, 1924-1953.

2.3G

700	**12**	**$a**	Neill, Edward D. **$q** (Edward Duffield), **$d** 1823-1893. **$t** Early French posts in Minnesota, [186-?]
730	**02**	**$a**	Gotcha! (Motion picture)

CHAPTER 3 HEADINGS FOR PERSONS

The examples in the text, shown here with USMARC coding, reflect the rules' incremental approach to heading construction. The Mary Cassatt example in 3.4B3 illustrates rule 3.4B3 only. In actual practice, use of all applicable rules might require further additions or modifications to the forms shown here, based on data found in the chief sources of information or reference sources, or as a result of conflict with another heading in the authority file. For example, the heading for Mary Cassatt that is established in the Library of Congress Name Authority File (LCNAF) is: Cassatt, Mary, 1844-1926. Construction of the heading required use of rule 3.4B3 *and* 3.14. Examples for rules 3.4B1-3.9, particularly, may be "incomplete" compared with the headings actually established in the LCNAF. In any case, if there is a heading already established in LCNAF, it should be used exactly that way in any catalog record.

3.4B1

100	**0-**	**$a**	Ram Gopal.

3.4B2

100	**1-**	**$a**	Chiang, Kai-shek.

3.4B3

100	**1-**	**$a**	Cassatt, Mary.

3.4B4

100	**1-**	**$a**	Leighton, Frederick Leighton, **$c** Baron.
100	**1-**	**$a**	Caradon, Hugh Foot, **$c** Baron.

3.5A

100	**1-**	**$a**	Bernhardt, Sarah.
100	**1-**	**$a**	Fitzgerald, Ella.
100	**1-**	**$a**	Ching, Francis K. W.
100	**1-**	**$a**	Q., Mike.

3.5B

100	**1-**	**$a**	Hus, Jan.
100	**1-**	**$a**	Ali, Muhammad.
100	**1-**	**$a**	X, Malcolm.

3.5C2

100	**2-**	**$a**	Lloyd George, David.
100	**1-**	**$a**	Fénelon, François de Salignac de la Mothe-
100	**2-**	**$a**	Machado de Assis, Joaquim Maria.

3.5C3

100	**2-**	**$a**	Day-Lewis, Cecil.
100	**2-**	**$a**	Henry-Bordeaux, Paule.

3.5C4

100	**2-**	**$a**	Johnson Smith, Geoffrey.
100	**2-**	**$a**	Hungry Wolf, Adolf.
100	**2-**	**$a**	Cotarelo y Mori, Emilio.
100	**1-**	**$a**	Silva, Ovidio Saraiva de Carvalho e.

3.5C5

100	**2-**	**$a**	Bonacci Brunamonti, Alinda.
100	**2-**	**$a**	Molina y Vedia de Bastianini, Delfina.
100	**1-**	**$a**	Stowe, Harriet Beecher.
100	**2-**	**$a**	Wang Ma, Hsi-ch'un.

3.5C6

100	**1-**	**$a**	Adams, John Crawford.
100	**1-**	**$a**	Lee, Joseph Jenkins.

3.5D1

100	**1-**	**$a**	De Morgan, Augustus.
100	**1-**	**$a**	De la Mare, Walter.
100	**1-**	**$a**	Du Maurier, Daphne.
100	**1-**	**$a**	Le Gallienne, Richard.
100	**1-**	**$a**	Van Buren, Martin.
100	**1-**	**$a**	Von Braun, Wernher.
100	**1-**	**$a**	Le Rouge, Gustave.
100	**1-**	**$a**	La Bruyère, René.
100	**1-**	**$a**	Du Méril, Édélestand Pontas.
100	**1-**	**$a**	Des Granges, Charles-Marc.

3.5D2

100	**1-**	**$a**	À Beckett, Gilbert Abbott.
100	**1-**	**$a**	Ap Rhys Price, Henry Edward.
100	**1-**	**$a**	Ben Maÿr, Berl.

3.5E1

100	**1-**	**$a**	FitzGerald, David.
100	**1-**	**$a**	MacDonald, William.
100	**1-**	**$a**	Debure, Guillaume.
100	**1-**	**$a**	Fon-Lampe, A. A.

3.5F1

100	**1-**	**$a**	Habsburg, Otto.
100	**1-**	**$a**	Hohenzollern, Franz Joseph, **$c** Fürst von.
100	**1-**	**$a**	Paris, Henri, **$c** comte de.
100	**1-**	**$a**	Wied, Maximilian, **$c** Prinz von.

3.6A

100	**1-**	**$a**	Byron, George Gordon Byron, **$c** Baron.
100	**1-**	**$a**	Macaulay, Thomas Babington Macaulay, **$c** Baron.
100	**1-**	**$a**	Nairne, Carolina Nairne, **$c** Baroness.

3.6A1

100	**2-**	**$a**	Russell of Liverpool, Edward Frederick Langley Russell, $c Baron.
100	**1-**	**$a**	Bracken, Brendan Bracken, $c Viscount.

3.6B2

100	**1-**	**$a**	Kames, Henry Home, $c Lord.

3.6B3

100	**1-**	**$a**	Caradon, Hugh Foot, $c Baron.
100	**2-**	**$a**	George-Brown, George Brown, $c Baron.
100	**2-**	**$a**	Hailsham of St. Marylebone, Quintin Hogg, $c Baron.

3.7A

100	**0-**	**$a**	John, $c the Baptist.
100	**0-**	**$a**	Leonardo, $c da Vinci.
100	**0-**	**$a**	John of the Cross.

3.7A2

100	**1-**	**$a**	Planudes, Maximus.
100	**1-**	**$a**	Helena, Maria.

3.8A

100	**0-**	**$a**	H. D.
100	**0-**	**$a**	A. de O.
100	**0-**	**$a**	B..., $c abbé de.
100	**0-**	**$a**	D. S., $c Master.

3.9A

100	**0-**	**$a**	Dr. X.
100	**0-**	**$a**	Father Time.
100	**0-**	**$a**	Pan Painter.
100	**0-**	**$a**	Mr. Fixit.
100	**0-**	**$a**	Buffalo Bill.
100	**0-**	**$a**	Typhoid Mary.
100	**0-**	**$a**	Poor Richard.
100	**1-**	**$a**	Other, A. N.
100	**0-**	**$a**	River $c (Writer)
100	**0-**	**$a**	Taj Mahal $c (Musician)

3.9B

100	**0-**	**$a**	Fannie, $c Cousin.
100	**0-**	**$a**	Jemima, $c Aunt.
100	**0-**	**$a**	Pierre, $c Chef.

3.10A

100	**1-**	**$a**	Bismarck, Otto, $c Fürst von.

3.10B

100	**1-**	**$a**	West, Rebecca, $c Dame.
100	**1-**	**$a**	Beecham, Thomas, $c Sir.
100	**1-**	**$a**	Gordon, George, $c Lord.

3.11A

100	**0-**	**$a**	Alban, **$c** Saint.
100	**0-**	**$a**	Teresa, **$c** of Avila, Saint.
100	**0-**	**$a**	Francis, **$c** of Assisi, Saint.
100	**1-**	**$a**	More, Thomas, **$c** Sir, Saint.
100	**1-**	**$a**	Seton, Elizabeth Ann, **$c** Saint.

3.11B

100	**0-**	**$a**	Augustine, **$c** Saint, Archbishop of Canterbury.
100	**0-**	**$a**	Augustine, **$c** Saint, Bishop of Hippo.

3.12A

100	**0-**	**$a**	Deidier, **$c** abbé.
100	**1-**	**$a**	Moses, **$c** Grandma.
100	**1-**	**$a**	Read, **$c** Miss.
100	**1-**	**$a**	D'Ambrosio.

3.12B

100	**1-**	**$a**	Ward, Humphry, **$c** Mrs.

3.13A1

100	**0-**	**$a**	Clovis, **$c** King of the Franks.
100	**0-**	**$a**	Hirohito, **$c** Emperor of Japan.
100	**0-**	**$a**	John **$c** King of England.
100	**0-**	**$a**	Jean, **$c** Grand Duke of Luxembourg.
100	**0-**	**$a**	Alfonso **$b** XIII, **$c** King of Spain.
100	**0-**	**$a**	Elizabeth **$b** II, **$c** Queen of Great Britain.
100	**0-**	**$a**	Victor Emmanuel **$b** II, **$c** King of Italy.
100	**0-**	**$a**	Gustaf **$b** I Vasa, **$c** King of Sweden.
100	**0-**	**$a**	Gustaf **$b** II Adolf, **$c** King of Sweden.

3.13A2

100	**0-**	**$a**	Louis **$b** IX, **$c** King of France.
100	**0-**	**$a**	Constantine **$b** I, **$c** Emperor of Rome.
100	**0-**	**$a**	Charles, **$c** Duke of Burgundy.

[*etc.*]

3.13A3

100	**0-**	**$a**	Philip, **$c** Prince, consort of Elizabeth II, Queen of Great Britain.
100	**0-**	**$a**	Albert, **$c** Prince Consort of Victoria, Queen of Great Britain.
100	**0-**	**$a**	Ingrid, **$c** Queen, consort of Frederick IX, King of Denmark.
100	**0-**	**$a**	Eleanor, **$c** of Aquitaine, Queen, consort of Henry II, King of England.

3.13A4

100	**0-**	**$a**	Carlos, **$c** Prince of Asturias.
100	**0-**	**$a**	Eulalia, **$c** Infanta of Spain.
100	**0-**	**$a**	Margaret, **$c** Princess, Countess of Snowdon.

100	**0-**	**$a**	Anne, **$c** Princess Royal, daughter of Elizabeth II, Queen of Great Britain.

3.13B

100	**0-**	**$a**	Pius **$b** XII, **$c** Pope.
100	**0-**	**$a**	Gregory **$b** I, **$c** Pope.
100	**0-**	**$a**	Clement **$b** VII, **$c** Antipope.

3.13C

100	**0-**	**$a**	Bēssariōn, **$c** Cardinal.
100	**0-**	**$a**	Dositheos, **$c** Patriarch of Jerusalem.
100	**0-**	**$a**	John, **$c** Bishop of Ephesus.
100	**0-**	**$a**	Platon, **$c** Metropolitan of Moscow.
100	**1-**	**$a**	Cushing, Richard, **$d** 1895-
100	**1-**	**$a**	Gibbons, James, **$d** 1834-1921.

3.14

100	**1-**	**$a**	Smith, John, **$d** 1924-
100	**1-**	**$a**	Smith, John, **$d** 1900 Jan 10-
100	**1-**	**$a**	Smith, John, **$d** 1900 Mar. 2-
100	**1-**	**$a**	Smith, John, **$d** 1837-1896.
100	**1-**	**$a**	Mantovani, **$d** 1905-1980.
100	**0-**	**$a**	Pliny, **$c** the Younger, **$d** 62-113.
100	**1-**	**$a**	Davies, W. H. **$q** (William Henry), **$d** 1871-1940.
100	**1-**	**$a**	Lindbergh, Charles A. **$q** (Charles August), **$d** 1859-1924.
100	**1-**	**$a**	Lindbergh, Charles A. **$q** (Charles Augustus), **$d** 1902-1974.
100	**1-**	**$a**	Torrance, Ell, **$d** 1844-1932.
100	**1-**	**$a**	Torrance, Ell, **$d** 1878-1940.
100	**1-**	**$a**	Smith, John, **$d** 1836 or 7-1896.
100	**1-**	**$a**	Smith, John, **$d** 1837?-1896.
100	**0-**	**$a**	Ovid, **$d** 43 B.C.-17 or 18 A.D.
100	**1-**	**$a**	Smith, John, **$d** ca. 1837-1896.
100	**1-**	**$a**	Smith, John, **$d** 1837-ca. 1896
100	**1-**	**$a**	Smith, John, **$d** ca. 1837-ca. 1896.
100	**1-**	**$a**	Smith, John, **$d** b. 1825.
100	**1-**	**$a**	Smith, John, **$d** d. 1859.
100	**1-**	**$a**	Johnson, Carl F., **$d** fl. 1893-1896.
100	**0-**	**$a**	Joannes, **$c** Diaconus, **$d** fl. 1226-1240.

3.15A

100	**1-**	**$a**	Flam, F. A. **$q** (Floyd A.)
100	**1-**	**$a**	Smith T. B. **$q** (T. Basil)
100	**1-**	**$a**	Wright, G. H. von **$q** (Georg Henrik), **$d** 1916-
100	**1-**	**$a**	Smith, Arthur D. **$q** (Arthur Dwight), **$d** 1907-
100	**1-**	**$a**	Bvindi, Francis A. A. L. **$q** (Francis A. A. Lovemore), **$d** 1955-
100	**2-**	**$a**	Rodríguez H., Guadalupe **$q** (Rodríguez Hernández)
100	**2-**	**$a**	González R., Pedro F. **$q** (Pedro Felipe González Rodríguez)
100	**0-**	**$a**	M. Alicia **$q** (Mary Alicia), **$c** Sister, S.C.N.

100 0- $a H. D. $q (Hilda Doolittle), $d 1886-1961.
100 1- $a Renfro, Roy E., $c Mrs.
100 1- $a Brownridge, Wm. $q (William)

3.16A

100 0- $a Johannes $c (Notary)
100 0- $a Thomas $c (Anglo-Norman poet)
100 0- $a Charles $c (Blacksmith of Wake County, N.C.)

3.16B

100 1- $a Brown, George, $c Captain.
100 1- $a Saur, Karl-Otto, $c Jr.
100 1- $a Baker, $c Miss, of Falls Church, Va.
100 1- $a Falkland, Leonard, $c Blacksmith of Elsah, Ill.
100 1- $a Stevens, Samuel, $c Ph. D.
100 0- $a T. H. $c (Merchant of York)
100 1- $a Dyer, Will, $c wool merchant.

CHAPTER 4 GEOGRAPHIC NAMES

While the rules in chapter 4 govern the formation of all geographic names, their tagging in a USMARC record depends on their use. If a geographic entity is the entry element in a corporate heading, it is considered to be part of that heading.

110 1- $a Québec (Province). $b Service de l'exploration géologique.

110 1- $a France. $b Cour d'appel (Caen)

110 1- $a Philadelphia (Pa.). $b Mayor.

Geographic names used as subject added entries are tagged as 651 fields, although the rules currently governing the indirect (geographic) subdivision of topical headings (650) usually do not permit the use of an AACR 2-based geographic subdivision.

651 -0 $a United States $x History $y Civil War, 1861-1865.

651 -0 $a Chicago (Ill.) $x Social life and customs.

but

650 -0 $a Universities and colleges $z Illinois $z Chicago.

Furthermore, in the *USMARC Format for Bibliographic Data*, published by the Library of Congress, there is a table in the introduction to the section on subject added entries (6XX) of problematic headings, many of which are geographic in nature. This list reflects tagging decisions made by the Library of Congress and must be consulted in the course of creating USMARC records containing these headings.

CHAPTER 5 HEADINGS FOR CORPORATE BODIES

5.1

110 2- $a Aslib.
110 2- $a Breitkopf & Härtel.

168

110 2- $a British Museum.
110 2- $a Carnegie Library of Pittsburgh.
110 2- $a Chartered Insurance Institute.
110 2- $a Light Fantastic Players.
110 2- $a MEDCOM.
110 2- $a Museum of American Folk Art.
110 2- $a Radio Society of Great Britain.
110 2- $a Royal Aeronautical Society.
110 2- $a University of Oxford.
110 2- $a Yale University.

5.2D

110 2- $a AFL-CIO.
110 2- $a American Philosophical Society.
110 2- $a Euratom.
110 2- $a Maryknoll Sisters.
110 2- $a Unesco.

5.3A

110 2- $a Société historique franco-américaine.
110 2- $a Canadian Committee on Cataloguing.
110 2- $a Schweizerische Landesbibliothek.
[*etc. The coding of most corporate names follows the pattern above. Examples of headings with additions, conference headings, and government headings follow.*]

5.4B

110 2- $a Apollo 11 (Spacecraft)
110 2- $a Bounty (Ship)
110 2- $a Franklin (Aircraft carrier)
110 2- $a Elks (Fraternal order)
110 2- $a Friedrich Witte (Firm)
[*etc.*]

110 2- $a Morgan and Morgan.
110 2- $a B. Morgan and D. Morgan (Firm)
110 2- $a Simon and Garfunkel
110 2- $a Ian and Sylvia
110 2- $a Red Sea (Restaurant : Washington, D.C.)
[*etc.*]

5.4C

110 2- $a Arlington Development Center (Arlington, Tex.)
[*etc.*]

110 2- $a National Endowment for the Arts (U.S.)
[*etc.*]

110 2- $a Rome Historical Society (Rome, N.Y.)
[*etc.*]

5.4C2

110 2- $a Republican Party (Ill.)
[*etc.*]

5.6B

110	**1-**	**$a**	Cork (Ireland : County)
110	**1-**	**$a**	Darmstadt (Germany : Landkreis)
110	**1-**	**$a**	New York (N.Y.)
110	**1-**	**$a**	Québec (Québec)

5.7B4

111	**2-**	**$a**	Conference on Machinability **$d** (1965 : **$c** London, England)
111	**2-**	**$a**	Symposium on Glaucoma **$d** (1966 : **$c** New Orleans, La.)
111	**2-**	**$a**	Louisiana Cancer Conference **$n** (1st : **$d** 1958 : **$c** New Orleans, La.)
111	**2-**	**$a**	Arden House Conference on Medicine and Anthropology **$d** (1961)

5.8B

111	**2-**	**$a**	Festival of Britain **$d** (1951 : **$c** London, England)
111	**2-**	**$a**	Biennale di Venezia **$n** (36th : **$d** 1972)
111	**2-**	**$a**	World's Columbian Exposition **$d** (1893 : **$c** Chicago, Ill.)
111	**2-**	**$a**	Expo 67 **$d** (1967 : **$c** Montréal, Québec)

5.9

110	**2-**	**$a**	Freemasons. **$b** Concordia Lodge, No. 13 (Baltimore, Md.)
110	**2-**	**$a**	Knights Templar (Masonic Order). **$b** Grand Commandery (Me.)
110	**2-**	**$a**	Daughters of the American Revolution. **$b** Mary Clap Wooster Chapter (New Haven, Conn.)
110	**2-**	**$a**	Psi Upsilon (Fraternity). **$b** Gamma Chapter (Amherst College)
110	**2-**	**$a**	Society of St. Vincent De Paul. **$b** Conference (Cathedral of St. John the Baptist (Savannah, Ga.))

5.10B

110	**2-**	**$a**	Unitarian Universalist Church (Silver Spring, Md.)
110	**2-**	**$a**	Santo Domingo (Monastery : Pamplona, Spain)
110	**2-**	**$a**	Saint James' Church (New York, N.Y. : Catholic)

5.11A

110	**2-**	**$a**	WCIA (Television station : Champaign, Ill.)
110	**2-**	**$a**	WQDR (Radio station : Raleigh, N.C.)

5.12

110	**2-**	**$a**	Ansco.
110	**2-**	**$a**	Association of College and Research Libraries.
110	**2-**	**$a**	BBC Symphony Orchestra.

5.13
(Type 1)

110	**2-**	**$a**	British Broadcasting Corporation. **$b** Engineering Division.
110	**2-**	**$a**	International Federation of Library Associations and Institutions. **$b** Section on Cataloguing.
110	**2-**	**$a**	Stanford University. **$b** Dept. of Civil Engineering.

5.13 (Type 2)

110 2- $a Association of State Universities and Land-Grant Colleges. $b Committee on Traffic Safety Research and Education.

110 2- $a International Council on Social Welfare. $b Canadian Committee.

110 2- $a University of Wales. $b University Commission.

110 2- $a Society of American Archivists. $b National Information Systems Task Force.

(Type 3)

110 2- $a American Dental Association. $b Research Institute.

110 2- $a Canadian Jewish Congress. $b Central Region.

110 2- $a Dartmouth College. $b Class of 1980.

(Type 4)

110 2- $a British Library. $b Collection Development.

110 2- $a Bell Canada. $b Corporate Public Relations.

(Type 5)

110 2- $a Syracuse University. $b College of Medicine.

110 2- $a Universität Wien. $b Institut für Österreichische Geschichtforschung.

110 2- $a University of California, Berkeley. $b University Art Museum.

(Type 6)

110 2- $a American Legion. $b Auxiliary.

110 2- $a Labour Party (Great Britain). $b Conference $n (72nd : $d 1972 : $c Blackpool, England)

110 2- $a United Methodist Church (U.S.). $b General Conference.

5.16

110 2- $a Republican Party (Mo.). $b State Committee.

110 2- $a Democratic Party (Tex.). $b State Convention $d (1857 : $c Waco, Tex.)

5.18
(Type 1)

110 1- $a Vermont. $b Dept. of Water Resources.

110 1- $a United States. $b Division of Wildlife Services.

(Type 2)

110 1- $a Australia. $b Bureau of Agricultural Economics.

110 1- $a United States. $b Bureau of Insular Affairs.

110 2- $a Royal Commission on Higher Education in New Brunswick.

(Type 3)

110 1- $a United States. $b National Labor Relations Board. $b Library.

110 1- $a Niger. $b Commissariat général au développement. $b Centre de documentation.

110 1- $a United States. $b Public Health Service. $b Region IX.

5.18 (Type 4)

110	1-	$a	Lower Saxony (Germany). $b Landesvermessung.
110	1-	$a	Canada. $b Ocean and Aquatic Sciences.

(Type 5),

110	1-	$a	Great Britain. $b Home Office.
110	1-	$a	Italy. $b Ministero del bilancio e della programmazione economica.

(Type 6)

110	1-	$a	Chicago (Ill.). $b City Council.
110	1-	$a	France. $b Assemblée nationale.
110	1-	$a	United States. $b Congress.

(Type 7)

110	1-	$a	Ontario. $b High Court of Justice.
110	1-	$a	United States. $b Supreme Court.

(Type 8)

110	1-	$a	Germany. $b Heer.
110	1-	$a	United States. $b Navy.

(Type 9)

110	1-	$a	Great Britain. $b Sovereign.
110	1-	$a	Montréal (Québec). $b Mayor.

(Type 10)

110	1-	$a	Canada. $b Embassy (U.S.)
110	1-	$a	Great Britain. $b Consulate (New York, N.Y.)

(Type 11)

110	1-	$a	Great Britain. $b Delegation to the United Nations.

5.19

110	1-	$a	Québec (Province). $b Service de l'exploration géologique.
110	1-	$a	United States. $b Aviation Forecast Branch.
110	1-	$a	Great Britain. $b Dept. of Employment. $b Solicitor's Office.

5.20B

110	1-	$a	United States. $b President (1953-1961 : Eisenhower)
110	1-	$a	Papal States. $b Sovereign (1846-1870 : Pius IX)

5.20C

110	1-	$a	Philadelphia (Pa.). $b Mayor.
110	1-	$a	United Nations. $b Secretary-General.

5.20D

110	1-	$a	Netherlands (Territory under German occupation, 1940-1945). $b Reichskommisar für die Besetzten Niederländischen Gebiete.
110	1-	$a	Germany (Territory under Allied occupation, 1945-1955 : U.S. Zone). $b Military Governor.

5.21A

110 **1-** **$a** Great Britain. **$b** Parliament. **$b** House of Commons.
110 **1-** **$a** United States. **$b** Congress. **$b** Senate.

5.21B

110 **1-** **$a** United States. **$b** Congress. **$b** House. **$b** Select Committee on Government Operations.

5.21C

110 **1-** **$a** United States. **$b** Congress. **$b** Senate. **$b** Committee on Foreign Affairs. **$b** Subcommittee on Canadian Affairs.

5.21D

110 **1-** **$a** United States. **$b** Congress **$n** (87th : **$d** 1961-1962). **$b** House.
110 **1-** **$a** United States. **$b** Congress **$n** (87th, 2nd session : **$d** 1962). **$b** House.

5.22A

110 **1-** **$a** Germany. **$b** Nationalversammlung (1919-1920)
110 **1-** **$a** New Hampshire. **$b** Constitutional Convention **$d** (1781)

5.23A

110 **1-** **$a** France. **$b** Cour d'appel (Caen)
110 **1-** **$a** United States. **$b** Court of Appeals (District of Columbia Circuit)
110 **1-** **$a** United States. **$b** District Court (Illinois : Northern District : Eastern Division)
110 **1-** **$a** California. **$b** Municipal Court (Los Angeles Judicial District)
110 **1-** **$a** United States. **$b** Attorney (District of Columbia)
110 **1-** **$a** Wisconsin. **$b** District Attorney (Milwaukee County)

5.23B

110 **1-** **$a** United States. **$b** Army. **$b** Court of Inquiry (Hall : 1863)

5.24A

110 **1-** **$a** United States. **$b** Marine Corps.
110 **1-** **$a** United States. **$b** Army. **$b** Corps of Engineers.
110 **1-** **$a** France. **$b** Armée. **$b** Régiment de dragons, 15e.
110 **1-** **$a** Germany. **$b** Heer. **$b** Panzerdivision, 11.
110 **1-** **$a** United States. **$b** Army. **$b** Ohio Infantry Regiment, 42nd (1861-1864)
110 **1-** **$a** United States. **$b** Army. **$b** Pennsylvania Cavalry Regiment, 6th (1861-1865)
110 **1-** **$a** Confederate States of America. **$b** Army. **$b** Tennessee Infantry Regiment, 19th.

5.24B

110 **1-** **$a** New York (State). **$b** Militia. **$b** Regiment of Artillery, 9th.

5.25

110	1-	$a	Germany. $b Gesandtschaft (Switzerland)
110	1-	$a	Yugoslavia. $b Poslantsvo (U.S.)
110	1-	$a	Great Britain. $b Consulate (Cairo, Egypt)

5.26

110	1-	$a	United States. $b Mission to the United Nations.
110	1-	$a	Uruguay. $b Delegación en las Naciones Unidas.
110	1-	$a	Ecuador. $b Segunda Delegación a la Conferencia Panamericana de Bellas Artes, 5th, 1949, Lima, Peru.

5.27A1

| 110 | 2- | $a | Catholic Church. $b Antilles Episcopal Conference. |
| 110 | 2- | $a | Society of Friends. $b Philadelphia Yearly Meeting. |

5.27A2

| 110 | 2- | $a | Catholic Church. $b Concilium Plenarium Americae Latinae $d (1899 : $c Rome, Italy) |
| 110 | 2- | $a | Catholic Church. $b Province of Mexico City. $b Concilio Provincial $n (3rd : $d 1585) |

5.27B1

| 110 | 2- | $a | Catholic Church. $b Diocese of Campos. $b Bishop (1949- : Mayer) |

5.27B2

| 110 | 2- | $a | Catholic Church. $b Pope (1878-1903 : Leo XIII) |

5.27C2

| 110 | 2- | $a | Church of England. $b Diocese of Ely. |
| 110 | 2- | $a | Episcopal Church. $b Diocese of Southern Virginia. |

CHAPTER 6 UNIFORM TITLES

Introduction

100	1-	$a	Dickens, Charles, $d 1812-1870.
240	00	$a	Martin Chuzzlewit
245	04	$a	The life and adventures of Martin Chuzzlewit.
600	10	$a	Dickens, Charles, $d 1812-1870. $t Martin Chuzzlewit.
100	1-	$a	Neill, Edward D. $q (Edward Duffield), $d 1823-1893.
245	00	$a	Papers, $f 1768-1931.
600	10	$a	Neill, Edward D. (Edward Duffield), $d 1823-1893. $t Papers, 1768-1931.
245	00	$a	Harkness collection, $f 1525-1651.
630	00	$a	Harkness collection, $f 1525-1651.

6.2

| 600 | 10 | $a | Sayers, Dorothy L. $q (Dorothy Leigh), $d 1893-1957. $t Busman's honeymoon (Novel) |

174

6.3

630	**00**	**$a**	Analecta anglicana.
600	**10**	**$a**	Kennedy, John F. **$q** (John Fitzgerald), **$d** 1917-1963. **$t** Profiles in courage.
600	**10**	**$a**	Whitman, Walt, **$d** 1819-1892. **$t** Leaves of grass.
610	**20**	**$a**	Minnesota Library Association. **$t** Records, 1891-1977.

6.4

130	**0-**	**$a**	Amos 'n' Andy (Radio program)
130	**0-**	**$a**	Mary Tyler Moore show (Television program)

6.5

630	**00**	**$a**	New York times (New York, N.Y. : 1857)
610	**20**	**$a**	Library of Congress. **$t** Annual report of the Librarian of Congress for the fiscal year ended 1988.
630	**00**	**$a**	MLA newsletter (Minnesota Library Association)

6.6

600	**10**	**$a**	Trudeau, G. B., **$d** 1948- **$t** Doonesbury (Comic strip)
130	**0-**	**$a**	Blondie (Comic strip)

6.7

630	**00**	**$a**	M*A*S*H (Motion picture)
630	**00**	**$a**	Miracle on 34th Street (Motion picture : 1947)

6.8

630	**00**	**$a**	dBase III plus (Computer program)

6.9B

130	**0-**	**$a**	Domesday book.
130	**0-**	**$a**	Book of Lismore.
110	**2-**	**$a**	British Library. **$k** Manuscript. **$n** Arundel 384.

6.10A

110	**1-**	**$a**	Great Britain.
240	**00**	**$a**	Laws, etc.
245	**00**	**$a**	Halsbury's statutes of England...
110	**1-**	**$a**	United States.
240	**00**	**$a**	Laws, etc.
245	**00**	**$a**	United States code...

6.10B

110	**1-**	**$a**	Great Britain.
240	**00**	**$a**	Field Monuments Act 1972

6.10C

610	**10**	**$a**	United States. **$t** Laws, etc.
610	**10**	**$a**	New Zealand. **$t** Copyright Act 1962.

6.11A

110	**1-**	**$a**	France.
240	**00**	**$a**	Treaties, etc. **$g** Great Britain
630	**00**	**$a**	Treaty of Utrecht **$d** (1713)

6.11B1

      110 **1-** **$a** Denmark.

      240 **00** **$a** Treaties, etc. **$g** Great Britain, **$d** 1966 Mar. 3

6.11B2

      630 **00** **$a** Treaty of Paris **$d** (1763)

      630 **00** **$a** Universal Copyright Convention **$d** (1952)

APPENDIX III

Tables of USMARC Equivalents for Descriptive Elements

Table III-A

The elements below are given in the order in which they appear in the cataloging manual.

Descriptive element	USMARC field/subfield
Title (1.1)	**245**
Formal title (1.1B1)	**245 $a**
Supplied title (1.1B2)	**245 $a**
Name element (1.1B3)	**245 $a**
Form of material (1.1B4)	**245 $k**
Date (1.1B5)	**245 $f**
Bulk dates (1.1B5)	**245 $g**
General material designation (GMD) (1.1C1)	**245 $h**
Parallel title (1.1D1)	**245 $b**
Other title information (1.1E)	**245 $b**
Statement of responsibility (1.1F)	**245 $c**
Edition (1.2)	**250**
Physical description (1.5)	**300**
Statement of extent (1.5B)	
(number only)	**300 $a**
(unit of measure)	**300 $f**
Other physical details (1.5C)	**300 $b**
Dimensions (1.5D)	**300 $c**
Notes	
Biographical/Historical (1.7B1)	**545**
Scope and content/Abstract (1.7B2)	**520**
Linking entry complexity (1.7B3)	**580**
(for simple *In* relationships only)	**773**
Additional physical form available (1.7B4)	**530 $a**
Availability source	**530 $b**
Availability conditions	**530 $c**
Order number	**530 $d**
Reproduction (1.7B5)	**533**
Type of reproduction	**533 $a**

Place of reproduction	**533 $b**
Agency responsible for reproduction	**533 $c**
Date of reproduction	**533 $d**
Physical description of reproduction	**533 $e**
Series statement (bibliographic)	**533 $f**
Location of originals/duplicates (1.7B6)	**535 $a**
Postal address	**535 $b**
Country of repository	**535 $c**
Telecommunications address	**535 $d**
Organization and arrangement (1.7B7)	**351**
Organization	**351 $a**
Arrangement	**351 $b**
Language (1.7B8)	**546 $a**
Alphabet, information code	**546 $b**
Provenance (1.7B9)	**561**
Immediate source of acquisition (1.7B10)	**541**
Source of acquisition	**541 $a**
Address	**541 $b**
Method of acquisition	**541 $c**
Date of acquisition	**541 $d**
Restrictions on access (1.7B11)	**506**
Terms governing access	**506 $a**
Jurisdiction	**506 $b**
Physical access provisions	**506 $c**
Authorized users	**506 $d**
Terms governing use and reproduction (1.7B12)	**540**
Terms governing use and reproduction	**540 $a**
Jurisdiction	**540 $b**
Authorization	**540 $c**
Authorized users	**540 $d**
Cumulative index/finding aids (1.7B13)	**555**
Citation/references (1.7B14)	**510**
Preferred citation of described materials (1.7B15)	**524**
Publications (1.7B16)	**581**
General note (1.7B17)	**500**

Personal name headings (3.4-3.16)	**100/600/700**
Personal name (3.4-3.9)	**$a**
Numeration (3.1A)	**$b**
Titles and other words associated	
with a name (3.10-3.12, 3.15-3.16)	**$c**
Dates associated with a name (3.14)	**$d**
Relator term (2.0D, 2.1A4, 2.1A6)	**$e**
Fuller form of name (3.15)	**$q**
Title of work in subheading (2.3F-2.3G,	
6.2-6.3, 6.5-6.6, 6.10C, 6.11B3)	**$t**
Corporate name headings (5.3-5.27)	**110/610/710**
Corporate name including	
most additions, and conferences	
entered subordinately (5.3-5.11) *or*	
Jurisdiction name as entry element (4.1-4.5)	**$a**
Subordinate unit (5.12-5.27)	**$b**
Number of part/section/meeting (5.7B2, 6.9)	**$n**
Date of meeting (5.7B3)	**$d**
Location of meeting (5.7B4)	**$c**
Conferences, congresses, meetings, etc.	**111/611/711**
Meeting name (5.7-5.8)	**$a**
Number of meeting (5.7B2)	**$n**
Date of meeting (5.7B3)	**$d**
Location of meeting (5.7B4)	**$c**
Subordinate unit (5.12-5.27)	**$e**
Uniform title headings (6.1-6.11)	
For main, subject, added entry heading	**130/630/730**
For uniform title heading following a main	
entry heading (100, 110, 111)	**240**

Table III-B

USMARC fields and subfields are given below in numerical order with citations to equivalent descriptive elements given in the right hand column.

USMARC fields/subfields	**Rule number(s)**
100/600/700 Personal name heading	3.4-3.16
$a Personal name	3.4-3.9
$b Numeration	3.1A
$c Titles and other words associated	
with a name	3.10-3.12,
	3.15-3.16
$d Dates associated with a name	3.14

$e	Relator term	2.0D, 2.1A4, 2.1A6
$t	Title of work in subheading	2.3F-2.3G 6.2-6.3, 6.5-6.6, 6.10C, 6.11B3

110/610/710 Corporate name heading — 5.3-5.27
- **$a** Corporate name (including most additions and conferences entered subordinately) — 5.3-5.11
  - (geographic names) — 4.1-4.5
- **$b** Subordinate unit — 5.12-5.27
- **$c** Location of meeting — 5.7B4
- **$d** Date of meeting — 5.7B3
- **$n** Number of part/section/meeting — 5.7B2, 6.9

111/611/711 Conferences, congresses, meetings, etc. — 5.7-5.8
- **$a** Meeting name — 5.7-5.8
- **$c** Location of meeting — 5.7B4
- **$d** Date of meeting — 5.7B3
- **$e** Subordinate unit — 5.12-5.27
- **$n** Number of meeting — 5.7B2

130/630/730 Uniform title headings — 6.1-6.11

240 Uniform title heading following main entry heading (100,110,111) — 6.1-6.11

245 Title proper — 1.1B
- **$a** Title — 1.1B1
- **$b** Parallel title — 1.1D
- **$b** Remainder of title — 1.1E
- **$c** Statement of responsibility — 1.1F
- **$f** Inclusive dates — 1.1B5
- **$g** Bulk dates — 1.1B5

250 Edition — 1.2

300 Physical description — 1.5
- **$a** Extent — 1.5B
- **$b** Other physical details — 1.5C
- **$c** Dimensions — 1.5D
- **$f** Type of unit — 1.5B

351 Organization and arrangement — 1.7B7

500 General note — 1.7B17

506	Restrictions on access note	1.7B11
510	Citation/references note	1.7B14
520	Summary, etc., scope note	1.7B2
524	Preferred citation note	1.7B15
530	Additional physical form available note	1.7B4
533	Reproduction note	1.7B5
535	Location of originals/duplicates note	1.7B6
540	Terms governing use and reproduction note	1.7B12
541	Immediate source of acquisition note	1.7B10
545	Biographical or historical note	1.7B1
546	Language note	1.7B8
555	Cumulative index/finding aids note	1.7B13
561	Provenance note	1.7B9
580	Linking entry complexity note	1.7B3
581	Publications note	1.7B16

INDEX

Change of name (cont.)
  jurisdiction or locality names (as additions), 5.4C6
Changes to established headings
  based on later evidence concerning predominant form of name, 5.2D
  when qualifier becomes inappropriate, 5.4C7
Channel Islands, place names, 4.4D
Chapters, of
  corporate bodies, 5.9 (*see also* Branches)
Charts, *see* Nontextual materials
Chief source of information, 0.11, 1.0B1, 2.0B
Chiefs of state, *see* Heads of state, etc.
Children of royal persons, additions to names, 3.13A4
China, place names, 4.2F
Choice of access points, 2
Chronological subdivisions
  corporate bodies, 5.13 (type 3)
  government agencies, 5.18 (type 3)
Church councils, 5.3C2 (note), 5.27A
Churches
  addition of place names, 5.10B
  additions to names not conveying idea of a church, 5.10A
  as corporate bodies, 2.1B1
  variant forms of names, 5.3G
Circa, use of abbreviation *ca.*
  in expressing inaccuracies and extrapolations, 1.0F
  with dates added to personal names, examples, 3.14
  with dates in titles, 1.1B5 (note)
Citations, preferred by custodian, 1.7B15 (*see also* Bibliographic citations)
Cities, towns, etc. (*see also* Place names)
  added to headings for consulates, 5.25
  added to headings for corporate bodies, 5.4C4
  added to names of smaller places, 4.4F2
Civil and criminal courts, 5.18 (type 7), 5.23
Civil War fighting units, *see* United States Civil War fighting units
Coast Guard stations, *see* Military installations
Codex manuscripts, 1.0A, 6.9
Collation, as an aspect of provenance, 1.7B9
Collections, archival
  definition, 1.0A
  entry under author, 2.1A5
  entry under title, 2.1C2
  family papers, entry, 2.1A3
  nonarchival corporate collections, entry under title, 2.1C4
  personal papers
    entry, 2.1A1-2.1A2
    titles, 1.1B4
  single form of material, titles, 1.1B4
  unknown origin or authorship, entry under title, 2.1C6

Collective description, characteristic of archival cataloging, 0.8, 0.10
Collectors of archival materials, 1.1B3
  added entries, 2.3C
  corporate collections, added entries, 2.3E
  designation in headings, 2.0D, 2.1A4
  name given in title, 1.1B3
Colonies, not differentiated from states with same name, 5.6B (*see also* Dependent territories)
Colons (*see also* Punctuation of description)
  in notes, 1.7A1
  in physical description, 1.5A1
  in titles, 1.1A1
  separating additions to names of conferences, 5.7B1
  separating additions to names of corporate bodies (multiple qualifiers), 5.4B
  with additions to names of governments, 5.6A
Colophons, as chief source of information, 1.0B1
Comics, uniform titles, 6.6
Commas (*see also* Punctuation of description)
  connecting additions to names of delegations to meetings, 5.26
  in additions to place names, 4.4A1
  preceding words or phrases associated with name not including surname, 3.7A1
  separating elements in personal names, 3.4B2-3.4B4
Commissions (*see also* Administrative subordination; Corporate bodies)
  corporate bodies, 5.13 (type 2)
  government agencies, 5.18 (type 2)
  to international and intergovernmental bodies, 5.18 (type 11), 5.26
Committees (*See also* Administrative subordination; Corporate bodies)
  corporate bodies, 5.13 (type 2)
  government agencies, 5.18 (type 2)
  joint, 5.15
  legislative bodies, 5.21B
Compact discs, statement of extent, 1.5B3
Compilers, designation in headings, 2.0D
Component branches of armed forces, 5.24A
Component parts (of collections, etc.)
  entry, 2.1
  linking hierarchical relationships, 1.7B3
Compound surnames, 3.5C
Computer files (*see also* Nontextual materials)
  as components of collections, 1.0A
  cataloging of, according to other rules, 1.0A
Computer programs, uniform titles, 6.8
Confederate military units, 5.24A
Conferences
  additions to names, 5.7B
  as corporate bodies, 2.1B1
  entered subordinately, 5.13 (type 6)
  omissions from names, 5.7A
  variant names, 5.3F

LCNAF, *see* Library of Congress Name Authority File

Ledgers, as examples of manuscripts, 1.0A

Legal documents, as examples of manuscripts, 1.0A

Legal materials *see* Laws, etc.; Treaties, etc.

Legations, 5.18 (type 10), 5.25

Legislative bodies, 5.18 (type 6), 5.21

Legislative committees or other subordinate units, 5.21B

Legislative subcommittees of U.S. Congress, U.S. states, 5.21C

Legislatures numbered consecutively, 5.21D

Lettered subdivisions
  corporate bodies, 5.13 (type 3)
  government agencies, 5.18 (type 3)

Letters (alphabetic), entry of personal names under, 3.8

Letters (manuscripts), 1.0A, 1.1B4, 1.1E1, 1.5B2, 1.7B2, 2.1A5 (*see also* Single manuscripts)

Levels of description, 0.12, 0.13

Levels of description, linking, 1.7B3

Levels of detail in description, 1.0D

Library of Congress Name Authority File (LCNAF), Part II Intro.

Library of Congress rule interpretations, Preface, 3.1B, 6.10A

Linear footage, *see* Extent, statement of

Linking entry complexity, notes on, 1.7B3

Literary rights restrictions, notes on, 1.7B12

Liturgical works, uniform titles, 6.1

Local churches, *see* Churches

Local place names
  added to names of conferences, 5.7B4
  added to names of corporate bodies, 5.4C1
  additions to identify, 4.4F2

Location, in titles, 1.1B4

London, place names, 4.2F

Lord, added to personal names, 3.10B

LS, definition and use, 1.1B4 (note)

Machine-readable data files,
  See Computer files

Main entries, 2.0A
  selected on basis of provenance, 2.1
  uniform titles, 6 (Intro.)

Malaysia
  constituent states, additions to, 5.6B
  place names, 4.4C1
  places on islands, 4.4F2

Manuscript(s) (*see also* Collectors of archival materials; Collections; Corporate records; Archival material)
  addressee, 1.1E1
  cartographic items, cataloging of, according to other rules, 1.0A
  contained within a collection, added entries, 2.3G

definition, 1.0A

individual, titles, 1.1B (examples)

maps, cataloging of, according to other rules, 1.0A

music, cataloging of, according to other rules, 1.0A

place of writing, 1.1E1

uniform titles, 6 (Intro.), 6.9

unknown origin or authorship, entry under title, 2.1C6

versions, 1.2A1

with formal titles, bound together, 1.1G

Maps (*see also* Nontextual materials)
  as components of collections, 1.0A
  as physical details, 1.5C1
  cataloging of, according to other rules, 1.0A

MARC AMC format,
  see USMARC AMC format

Marchionesses, marquesses, *see* Titles of honor, nobility, address, etc.

Marines, *see* Armed forces

Marks of omission, *see* Omission, marks of

Married women
  addition of terms of address to names, 3.12B
  forenames in parentheses, 3.2A
  identified by husband's name, fuller forms of husband's name not added, 3.15A (5)
  identified only by husband's name, 3.12B
  surname consisting of surname before marriage and husband's surname, 3.5C5

Material specific details area, not defined for archival materials, 1.3

Measurement of extent, *see* Extent, statement of

Medieval manuscripts, *see* Codex manuscripts

Meetings, *see* Conferences

Metropolitans, *see* Bishops, etc.

Microfiches, 1.5B3 (*see also* Microforms)

Microfilm cassettes, 1.5B3, 1.5D3 (*see also* Microforms)

Microforms
  as reproductions, 1.7B5
  available in addition to originals, 1.7B4
  cataloging problems, 1.7B6 (bold note)
  dimensions, 1.5D3
  polarity (positive, negative), 1.5C1
  statement of extent, 1.5B3
  titles, 1.1B1

Microopaques, 1.5D3 (*see also* Microforms)

Military courts, ad hoc, 5.23B

Military installations, treated as local places, 4.2G

Militia, *see* Armed forces

Minimum level of detail in description, 1.0D

Ministries, government, 5.18 (type 5) (*see also* Administrative divisions, etc.)

Minutes, as examples of manuscripts, 1.0A

Missions
  papal diplomatic, 5.27D

Sacer, omitted from headings, 5.27C4
Sacred scriptures, uniform titles, 6 (Intro.)
Saint vs. *St.* in place names, 4.2E2
Saints, 3.11A
Scope and content of described materials, notes concerning, 1.7B2
Scope of rules, Preface, 0.1, 0.3, 0.4, 0.5, 0.6
Scotland
    county or region name, additions to, 5.6B
    place names, 4.4D
Scottish Court of Session, judges of, 3.6B2
Scriptures, *see* Sacred scriptures
Secondary entries, *see* Added entries
Sections (*see also* Administrative divisions, etc.)
    corporate bodies, 5.13 (type 1)
    government agencies, 5.18 (type 1)
"See" references, explanation of, Part II Intro.
Semicolon, use of (*see also* Punctuation of description)
    in notes, 1.7A1
    in physical description, 1.5A1
    in statement of responsibility, 1.1A1
    in statements of responsibility associated with editions, 1.2A2
Separate bibliographic identity, 3.2B2
Series (archival)
    definition, 1.0A
    titles, 1.1B4
Series (bibliographic)
    for reproductions, 1.7B5
    not defined for archival materials, 1.6
Series descriptions, *see* Finding aids
Session numbers, additions to headings for legislatures, 5.21D
Shelf lists, *see* Finding aids
Ships
    abbreviations omitted from names, 5.5B3
    as corporate bodies, 2.1B1
    general designations added to names, 5.4B
sic, use of, 1.0F
Signers of documents, added entries, 2.1B5
Single form of material collections, titles, 1.1B4
Single manuscripts (*see also* Letters)
    abstract of content, 1.7B2
    chief source of information, 1.0B1
    choice of access points, 2.1A5, 2.1A6, 2.1B5
    date, 1.1B5
    dimensions, 1.5D
    statement of extent, 1.5B2
    statement of responsibility, 1.1F
Sir, added to personal names, 3.10B
Size, of entire collection, *see* Extent, statement of
Size, of items, containers, etc., 1.5D
Slash, diagonal, *see* Punctuation of description
Societies, *see* Corporate bodies; Religious orders and societies
Sound recordings, *see* Nontextual materials

Source of acquisition of archival materials, notes on, 1.7B10
Source of title, notes on, 1.7B17
Sources
    for determining access points, 2.0B
    for determining form of name of corporate body, 5.1
    for determining name by which person is commonly known, 3.1B
    for determining place names, 4.2C
    of information for description, 0.11, 1.0B
South Africa, place names for homelands, 4.4E1
South Korea, place names, 4.2F
Soviet Union
    constituent republics, additions to, 5.6B
    place names, 4.4C1
    place names of constituent republics, 4.2F
    places on islands, 4.4F2
    preferred form of place name, 4.2A
Spacecraft, as corporate bodies, 2.1B1
Spacing
    in names of corporate bodies containing initials, 5.1
    in personal name headings, 3.1B
    with prescribed punctuation, 1.0C
Span dates, *see* Inclusive dates
Speeches, as examples of manuscripts, 1.0A
Spelling errors, correction of, in transcribed data, 1.0F
Spelling variations, in names of corporate bodies, 5.2C
Square brackets
    for interpolations or extrapolations, 1.0C
    not used for supplied titles, 0.10
    with conjectural data or corrections, 1.0F
    with conjectural dates, 1.1B5
    with description replacing unreproducible symbols, 1.0E
    with edition statements, 1.2B3
    with ongoing dates, 1.1B5
    with uniform titles, 6.1
Standards for archival description, Preface
State (meaning national), in names of government bodies at the national level, 5.18 (type 3)
State and local elements of American political parties, 5.16
State militia, *see* Armed forces
State universities (U.S.), names containing name of statewide system, 5.13 (type 6, exclusion)
Statement of extent, *see* Extent, statement of
Statements of responsibility, 1.1F (*see also* Responsibility)
    relating to an edition, 1.2C
States
    added to corporate names, 5.4C2
    added to smaller place names, 4.4C2
    additions to names of, 5.6B